VGM Opportunities Series

OPPORTUNITIES IN **SPECIAL EDUCATION CAREERS**

Robert Connelly

Foreword by
Janis D. Flint-Ferguson
Assistant Professor of Education and English
Gordon College, Wenham, Massachusetts

VGM Career Horizons
a division of *NTC Publishing Group*
Lincolnwood, Illinois USA

Cover Photo Credits:

Clockwise from upper left: Special Olympics; National Easter Seal Society; American Occupational Therapy Association; National FFA Organization.

Library of Congress Cataloging–in–Publication Data

Connelly, Robert
    Opportunities in special education careers / Robert Connelly.
        p.   cm — (VGM opportunities series)
    Includes bibliographical references.
    ISBN 0–8442–4425–2 (hard) — ISBN 0–8442–4426–0 (soft)
    1. Special education teachers—Vocational guidance—United States.
I. Title. II. Series.
LC3981.C664   1995
371.9—dc20   94–49079
                                                              CIP

Published by VGM Career Horizons, a division of NTC Publishing Group
4255 West Touhy Avenue
Lincolnwood (Chicago), Illinois 60646-1975, U.S.A.
© 1995 by NTC Publishing Group. All rights reserved.
No part of this book may be reproduced, stored in a retrieval
system, or transmitted in any form or by any means,
electronic, mechanical, photocopying, recording or otherwise,
without the prior permission of NTC Publishing Group.
Manufactured in the United States of America.

5 6 7 8 9 0 VP 9 8 7 6 5 4 3 2 1

CONTENTS

ABOUT THE AUTHOR

Bob Connelly is director of a program for high school dropouts in the northwest suburbs of Chicago. Mr. Connelly earned his bachelor's and master's degrees in education from Northern Illinois University, where he studied foundations of education under the direction of Dr. Nolan Armstrong. Mr. Connelly has presented numerous papers on serving at-risk youth at state and national conferences, and he is the former editor of *Alternative Education: The Journal of the Illinois Alternative Education Association.*

FOREWORD

"I touch the future; I teach." Several years ago this was the tag line on an invitation to young professionals to consider the field of education. In another advertising campaign, NFL football players and popular television personalities tell the audience about the teacher who changed their lives. Although these romantic images of teaching may do nothing for filling teacher preparation courses, and despite their uncompromising pull on the heartstrings, they are nonetheless a reality. Teachers touch the future by influencing the lives of young people in their classes; teachers open new worlds of ideas and introduce a realm of possibilities to their students. Such realities are both the allure and the responsibility of the profession, and nowhere in education is it more true than in special education.

All teachers carry the weight of the future on their shoulders. All teachers are responsible for teaching life skills as well as developing the attitudes of lifelong learners. All teachers struggle with a curriculum and administration that at times seem out of touch with what really happens in the classroom. But special education teachers do it daily.

What's so special about special education? In a word, everything—which is why we need committed professionals in our schools. Teachers at all levels of education are familiar with the developmental range of the age they teach, but in special education this is a core requirement on which all else depends. Special education teachers must individualize curriculum and instruction for each student they see. They are counselor and cheerleader, coach and facilitator. And, when classroom teachers need to include students who have difficulty learning or exhibit behavioral problems, they turn to special education professionals.

We in the "regular" classrooms rely on the wisdom and experience of special education teachers and administrators to reach those students who might otherwise be lost to us. Special education is not a field for the fainthearted. This is not a place for do-gooders who only love the children and feel sorry for their problems. This is a field that requires strength of conviction in order to meet the demands that daily confront students and programs.

Education is not a singular activity; it takes a school, indeed an entire community, of dedicated personnel to affect the future. Within that school special education has become a vital link in the educational process. Without special education we could not be so confident of touching the future generations of our world. We need "special" educators to meet the challenges of special education and enable us all—whatever our strengths or disabilities—to touch the future.

Janis D. Flint-Ferguson
Assistant Professor of Education and English
Gordon College, Wenham, Massachusetts

INTRODUCTION

"But you have to remember that education is a service profession, and in a service profession, your status depends on that status of your clients. That's why professors have more status than high school teachers, and high school teachers have more status than kindergarten teachers. Nobody says it's fair, but that's how the system works. If you choose a career in special education, choose it because you want to serve people who need your help. If status is important to you, find another vocation."

> Dr. Nolan Armstrong
> Professor of Education
> Northern Illinois University

This is one of the most exciting times in the history of special education. Since 1975 all students in the United States, regardless of their handicap, have been entitled to a free public education in the least restrictive environment possible. The landmark Public Law 94–142 marks a high point in the evolution of attitudes about special needs students, attitudes that have ranged from viewing handicaps as a curse from God, a punishment for a moral lapse, or the result of degenerate immigrants fouling the gene pool. Public Law 94–142, the court cases that grew out of the law, and the Americans with Disabilities Act are all based on the idea that people with handicaps can learn, and that they are entitled to take as large a part in mainstream life as they can manage. Whether

ix

young people have mild or profound disabilities, they can benefit from education and socialization. They need to be included in mainstream programs as much as possible. The growth of special education services expands opportunities for young people; it also expands career opportunities for teachers and support personnel who want to help young people reach their maximum potential.

The term "special education" is used to describe the education program that is specially designed for students with handicaps that make it nearly impossible for them to function in a traditional classroom. These children need a program that diagnoses the educational problem, plans activities that will either help the student overcome the problem or compensate for it, and assesses their progress. This program is called an individualized educational program (or IEP), and it is the cornerstone of special education.

One of the greatest frustrations that students, teachers, and parents have faced is the segregation of students with special needs out of mainstream education. School boards and educators argued that pulling these students out of their home schools and transporting them to special education centers would be the most effective way to educate them. Segregating special needs students may have been efficient, but in doing so these students suffered losses, including the opportunity to socialize with mainstream students, the sense of belonging to a neighborhood school, and the opportunity to attend school with children from their own neighborhood.

Fortunately, schools in the United States and Canada are moving toward the inclusion of students with special needs in mainstream schools. The movement toward including these students will remedy many of the lost opportunities. Inclusion will permit special needs students to attend schools in their neighborhoods and to work with friends from their area. In addition, it will change the responsibilities and expectations for both mainstream as well as special education teachers. These changes may require special education teachers to work either as consultants or directly with small groups of students in mainstream schools. But no matter how the process of inclusion evolves, it will create new opportunities for both students and teachers.

Although teaching is the most visible career in special education, there are many other careers for people who want to help special needs students. This book describes careers in nursing, school social work, psychiatry, audiology, physical therapy, and the areas of specialization in teaching. Each job description includes an interview with a practicing professional, information on the skills and training needed to enter the field, and information on salaries and opportunities for people who work in the field.

You will also find information on developing effective resumes and cover letters and using student teaching or clinical experiences to make contacts and obtain meaningful volunteer and work experience. Finally, because an interview is one of the major steps in obtaining employment, interview strategies are discussed.

The appendices list resources that will help you expand your job search. The resources include directories of colleges that offer degree programs in special education and directories of public and private schools in the United States and Canada. Directories of hospitals, residential substance abuse programs, community programs, and correctional institutions that may offer education are also included.

Special education is a challenging but deeply rewarding field that requires intensive training and a genuine commitment to education. Those people who are drawn to this field, who train for it, and who enter the profession have my deepest respect.

CHAPTER 1

CAREERS IN COUNSELING

SCHOOL SOCIAL WORKER

Barb Hoferle is a school social worker at Rolling Meadows High School in Rolling Meadows, Illinois.

What interests or events led you into the field of social work?

My father held political office in our town and was often involved in charitable works. I also think that coming of age during the 1960s had a lot to do with my interest in social work. Possibly my Catholic education was of some significance.

Would you recommend a career in social work to someone you care about?

Yes, I would. The work is rewarding as well as challenging. You also have flexibility to move between schools, hospitals, or private practice.

How would you describe a typical workday? What kinds of activities tend to dominate your day?

There is a lot of variety. I write social histories, I counsel kids individually and in groups, I do crisis intervention, confer with staff, and consult with teachers.

What part of your education or work experience was the most valuable in terms of helping you to become a successful, effective social worker?

Probably my internship and my work in the field taught me the most. I was also involved in my own therapy for a while, and that was very helpful.

If you could change anything about your job, what would it be?

It would be nice not to have the pressure of writing sixty social histories a year so I could do more direct work with kids. I would also like to teach at the college level.

What is your greatest challenge as a school social worker?

Not getting burned out. I have used various strategies over the years to deal with this problem.

What is the most rewarding part of your job?

Working with students and parents. I also enjoy working with social work interns.

If you could give one piece of advice to someone who is about to enter this field, what would it be?

Get involved in your own therapy. It is crucial that you know yourself fairly well in order to work with others.

School social workers help students who have personal problems that interfere with their ability to do well in school. Many of the issues that these students face may be considered crisis issues, such as physical or sexual abuse, substance abuse, eating disorders, or depression. School social workers provide counseling to groups of students and to individuals. They work with state and local welfare officials trying to provide services that students may need. Social workers also intervene in dysfunctional family situations that threaten a child's progress at school.

One important responsibility that school social workers have is to write social histories for students who are being considered for special education services. Social workers also help students with physical or mental handicaps return to "mainstream" classes by working with teachers and by making sure that the students are not overwhelmed by school work. School social workers provide group sessions that help students develop social skills. They also provide emotional support during a difficult time in their student's lives.

Although school social work is a very challenging field, many people are drawn to it because they enjoy working with young people, and they feel a great sense of achievement when they are able to help young people overcome terrible difficulties. School social workers are professionals who need minimal day-to-day supervision. They have a great deal of discretion when it comes to setting up their daily schedule. Although the work is difficult, school social workers normally work the same hours and days as classroom teachers. Thus they have the opportunity to enjoy school vacations, which provide time for family obligations, professional growth, and a private caseload. School social workers are normally paid on the same salary schedule as classroom teachers, so wages will vary from one school district to another. In general, school social workers earn between $23,000 and $36,000 a year.

The greatest disadvantage of a career in school social work is stress. Many students have problems that are so severe that they cannot be solved. Many students have home lives that are so dysfunctional that a social worker will not be able to provide much help. The severity of these problems can lead a social worker to despair. As school budgets tighten, the caseload for social workers increases, as does the load of paperwork that social workers are responsible for.

The conflict between the need to provide direct counseling services and the need to complete paperwork and attend meetings also creates stress. With limited time and limited resources, it is sometimes difficult to prioritize needs.

There is no career ladder for school social workers. Once hired, they may come to enjoy a great deal of recognition within their school district, or even at the state or national level, but it is unlikely that the recognition will change their job description.

Effective school social workers like students and enjoy working in a school atmosphere. They need good listening skills because they need to pick up on nuances of speech and meaning. School social workers need excellent communication skills because they deal with students, parents, teachers, and administrators. Although social workers must bring a level of empathy and compassion to their jobs, they must also maintain enough scientific objectivity to be able to offer solutions and make referrals. Because of the serious emotional demands of this job, school social workers need to be mature and emotionally centered people.

Although it might be possible to find a job with a bachelor's degree in social work, sociology, or psychology, nearly every school district requires a master's degree in social work as a minimum requirement for employment. Forty-eight states and the District of Columbia require that school social workers be licensed, and provincial licensing is also a requirement in Canada. As of 1990, 438,000 people have careers in social work.

The federal government estimates that the demand for social workers will grow faster than the workforce in general through the year 2005 due to older social workers who are retiring and an increasing demand for social workers in response to increasing social problems. The demand for school social workers will reflect these trends, but as always school staffing will be shaped by state and local funding for education.

SCHOOL PSYCHOLOGIST

Ken Holliday is a school psychologist at Rolling Meadows High School in Rolling Meadows, Illinois.

What interests or events led you into the field of psychology?

A love of people and inspiration from a college professor, as well as support from a variety of other people.

Would you recommend a career in school psychology to someone you care about?

Yes, although the education funding issue casts a shadow over all careers in education.

How would you describe a typical workday? What kind of activities tend to dominate your day?

I spend a lot of time on emergency and crisis resolution. I also am heavily involved in group work, individual counseling, staff consultation, and support. Much of my time is spent on screenings for special education services and on psychological evaluations.

If you could change anything about your job, what would it be?

I would like to see us focus more time and energy on helping to support and refine school systems that show good education results and provide satisfied, productive students.

What is your greatest challenge as a school psychologist?

Dealing with non-research based, pseudo change in education.

What is the most rewarding part of your job?

Seeing positive growth and happiness in the people I work with.

What part of your education or work experience was most valuable in terms of helping you to become a successful and effective school psychologist?

An undergraduate course I took in learning helped me a lot, and my experience working with a behavior modification program at Peoria State Hospital was very helpful.

If you could give one piece of advice to someone who is about to enter this field, what would it be?

Enter the field with a Ph.D. This degree opens options that otherwise will not be there for you.

School psychologists provide many different services for students. Part of a school psychologist's role is to provide therapy for students who need help. School psychologists provide individual counseling for students who are working through some difficult problems, such as chemical dependency, physical or sexual abuse, or eating disorders. Psychologists also run issue-specific group therapy sessions, such as groups for children of alcoholics. In a time of crisis, when a sudden death or disaster strikes the school community, the school psychologist becomes the leader who coordinates the school's efforts to provide help for students and staff who need it.

The school psychologist is also responsible for testing students who may need special education services. In addition to administering and evaluating tests, the school psychologist develops psychological evaluations of students who may need special services to help them deal with learning or behavior problems. As part of this evaluation, the school psychologist needs to interview students and their families. The school psychologist also may need to observe students in the classroom. After developing an evaluation, the school psychologist participates in screenings and multidisciplinary staffings to help determine the most appropriate placement for students in question.

When asked about their job satisfaction, school psychologists say that they like their jobs because they have the opportunity to help students at a time when the students really need help. They feel a great sense of achievement when they are able to help students resolve difficult issues in their lives.

There are other rewards for school psychologists as well. As professionals, psychologists have a great deal of control over their work day. They work with students individually or in small groups without the pressure of grades or academic deadlines. School psychologists are often paid on the same salary schedule as teachers, which can range from $26,000 to $55,000 a year. In some communities, the salaries can be much higher. A school psychologist works the same days as the teaching staff and enjoys the same winter, spring, and summer vacations that teachers and students do. This vacation time allows the school psychologist time for family commitments or for professional growth. Some school psychologists also use this time to develop their own private practices in psychology.

In spite of these advantages, school psychology can be a very stressful career. The students they serve often need help with very serious problems, such as physical abuse, sexual abuse, alcoholism, drug abuse, homelessness, eating disorders, and other issues. At times it is difficult to get help from appropriate social agencies, and at times students have problems that are simply insurmountable. Teaching colleagues may demand that the school psychologist "Get this kid out of my classroom!" by recommending special education placement, even when the placement may not be appropriate. Parents may vent their own frustrations with their child's problems on the school and the psychologist. Budget cuts may increase caseloads to a point where the school psychologist may not be able to give students the attention they need.

Effective school psychologists have strong observation and communication skills. School psychologists need to be good listeners, and they need to communicate easily with parents, teachers, students, and school administrators. They need to project an image of optimism and confidence and have the ability to instill confidence in students. Psychologists need to be empathetic and compassionate, but they also must be objective enough to assess problems and work on solutions.

Preparation is critical to a successful career in school psychology. People who are interested in this field will need a bachelor's degree in psychology followed by at least two more years work in graduate school. The minimum requirement for this field is a master's degree in psychology, and career opportunities improve for people who enter this field with a Ph.D. in psychology. A Ph.D. will require an additional three years of study and will involve some kind of clinical experience, working under the supervision of a psychologist. School psychologists are licensed by the province or state in which they work. Licensing and certification requirements will vary from state to state. School psychologists with five years of experience may take the qualifying examination for a certificate of competence from the American Board of Professional Psychology.

The United States Department of Labor estimates that the number of jobs in psychology will grow faster than the average for the whole economy through the year 2005 as schools, hospitals, and businesses respond to the problems of chemical and physical abuse in our society. Jobs in individual school districts will continue to depend on enrollment and school funding, issues that will vary from one school district to another.

CHAPTER 2

CAREERS WITH THE PHYSICALLY IMPAIRED

PHYSICAL THERAPIST

Billie Tucker is a physical therapist at Palatine High School in Palatine Illinois.

What made you decide to enter the field of physical therapy?

I always wanted to be a physical therapist, even before I really knew what it was. I remember reading *Karen* when I was in fifth grade, and that made a big impression on me.

Would you recommend this career to someone you care about?

Absolutely. This is a wide-open job market and one of the best opportunities for people who want to work with other people. Physical therapists have a lot of choices about where they want to work and what age group they want to work with. This is a very challenging job, but it is never boring. There are almost constant changes.

What academic experience or work experience was most valuable in helping you become a successful and effective physical therapist?

One of my best experiences was working with children during my clinical rotation in pediatrics.

How would you describe a typical workday? What kinds of activities tend to dominate your day?

I work with students all day on a one-to-one basis. I help students work on exercises, ambulation, gait training, and mobility training. I spend a lot of time helping families get equipment that they need. I also work as a liaison between families, physicians, and hospitals. I also visit other schools and evaluate students for possible services.

What is the most rewarding part of your job?

Having the opportunity to help students achieve maximum independence by the time they graduate. I am also very happy to be able to help students recognize their abilities as opposed to their disabilities. These students need help with their physical problems, and they need help developing problem-solving skills. They also need to learn where they can go for help once they are out of school.

If you could give some advice to someone who is about to enter this field, what would it be?

People who are attracted to this job must be aware that physical therapy is an academically challenging program. Students who want to major in this field need a strong background in math and science. Most physical therapy programs have fairly limited enrollment, so they are very competitive.

Physical therapists work with people who need help regaining their mobility after an illness or an accident. In cases where the illness or injury is so severe that the patient will never be mobile, physical therapists help the patient relieve pain and limit the permanent damage that occurs as muscles atrophy. School districts and special education programs employ physical therapists to help children with physical handicaps, so these children can take part in classroom activities.

Physical therapists evaluate a patient's medical history and then test the patient's nerves, muscle strength, and range of motion. Once an assessment has been made, the physical therapist develops a treatment plan and begins treatments. These treatments may include exercises, thermal therapy, hydrotherapy, and deep muscle massage.

Physical therapists must keep accurate records of their patient's progress, and they need to be able to adapt these treatment plans to meet the patient's needs. Physical therapists who work in schools often spend a great deal of time helping students with prosthetic devices and supports, so the students will be able to sit, read, or write comfortably.

Physical therapy can be a very rewarding profession. Effective physical therapists can make a tremendous difference in the quality of a patient's life. Physical therapists who work in schools will enjoy the same school holidays and extended summer vacations that teachers in other areas do. The national average salary for physical therapists is $40,000 a year, although individual school districts or special education cooperatives may pay much higher salaries.

Physical therapists sometimes describe their work as frustrating because patients tend to make very slow progress. Physical therapists who work for school districts have the additional challenge of working with children who are going through a very painful and demanding time in their lives. The contrast between the image that we all have of childhood as a happy, carefree time and the actual suffering of these children can be very stressing.

Physical therapists need to bring many skills to their jobs. They must develop strong skills as therapists, and they must be willing to spend several hours a week keeping up with the new developments in physical therapy reported in the medical literature in their field. In addition to their medical skills, therapists need to develop communication skills that will enable them to understand and interpret information for their patients. Therapists need to deal with patients who are depressed by their situation. Physical therapists must be supportive and optimistic. Because of the draining nature of their work, physical therapists must be emotionally stable and responsible people. They must be able to put their own lives on hold while they attend to their patient's needs.

People who are interested in a career in physical therapy must earn a bachelor's degree in that area from an accredited university. Many school districts require a master's degree as an absolute minimum for employment. In addition to course work, physical therapists must complete a supervised clinical experience in a school or hospital. All states and provinces require prospective therapists to pass a licensing exam before they can be licensed to practice.

Most experts in education predict that job opportunities for physical therapists will continue to grow throughout the end of this century as medical advances make it possible for severely injured or ill children to attend school and as school districts include more special needs children in their programs. Job opportunities will also expand as an aging workforce retires.

TEACHER OF STUDENTS WHO ARE HEARING IMPAIRED

Gail Bedessen is a teacher of students who are hearing impaired at John Hersey High School in Arlington Heights, Illinois.

What made you interested in working with students who are hearing impaired?

I majored in speech and language pathology in college. One of my classmates was hearing impaired, and I was fascinated by the beauty of American Sign Language.

Would you recommend a career in this area to someone you care about?

I love working with hearing-impaired students. But to be successful in this field, you have to love people, and you have to love the process of communication. You also need to be creative and flexible.

How would you describe a typical day as a teacher of students who are hearing impaired? What kinds of activities tend to dominate your day?

I teach five different academic subjects to hearing-impaired students, so I have five preps a day, and that demands a lot of time. In addition to my academic work, I am the case manager for a number of students, and I interpret for them. In the course of one school day, I fill several different roles for my students.

If you could change one part of your job, what would it be?

I spend a lot of time teaching people in the community about deaf education. I wish there was a greater level of understanding about the culture of deaf people in the hearing community.

What do you view as the most rewarding part of your job?

The best part of my job is the opportunity to develop long-term relationships with my students. Our classes are small; sometimes we only have five students to each class. I work with the same students for three or four years, and I often have the same students in class for several periods a day. It is challenging, but I love it.

If you could give a piece of advice to someone who is about to enter this field, what would it be?

You need to immerse yourself in American Sign Language and in the culture of deaf people.

The process of sharing spoken information is so common that most people take it completely for granted. Whether it occurs as an informal social exchange or in the form of a structured event, like a lecture, we are used to listening for messages, sorting out background noise, and focusing on the information that we need. Students who are hearing impaired are at a tremendous disadvantage because they have been excluded from this informal education. Teachers who work with the hearing impaired need to help them understand the sounds and meanings of the words that make up our spoken language, and they must help students master the skills they need to create those sounds. In order to meet these goals, teachers work on auditory training, amplifying sounds so students can make the best use of the hearing that they have. Students learn to distinguish between background noise and communication. Teachers of students who are hearing impaired also teach speech reading, so students read lips and interpret facial expressions and gestures to understand what people are saying. In addition, these teachers teach sign language and finger spelling as communication tools.

One of the most challenging aspects of this career is the process of teaching students how to create the sounds that make up our spoken language. Teachers must be able to demonstrate the movement of the mouth and tongue and the breath control needed to create speech. In addition to teaching these important skills, teachers of students who are hearing impaired must teach all of the academic subjects that their students need to master. Although this is a difficult career, it is an important one. Unless these students have access to auditory training and develop skills in speech reading and sign, they will always be isolated from the hearing community. Teachers who choose this profession value communication and want to share their skills with others. Although teachers of students who are hearing impaired have a wide range of responsibilities, they work with small groups of students, which makes for an informal class and allows for a great deal of teacher/student interaction.

Teachers in this field earn between $25,000 and $40,000 a year, depending on their level of education, their years of experience, and the salary scale of their individual school district. Teachers generally work a ten-month school year and benefit from school holidays and an extended summer vacation, both of which allow time for professional and personal growth.

Students who are hearing impaired are often deeply frustrated by their inability to communicate feelings and ideas to people who hear. Teachers who work with hearing-impaired students sometimes share this frustration. Some students also have problems with their social development because they have been excluded from so much day-to-day informal communication. The time and effort needed to help students develop social skills can represent an additional burden for the teacher. Although practitioners agree that teaching hearing-impaired students is rewarding work, it is also painstaking and repetitive work. Progress can be extremely slow, and the dual nature of the job—the need to teach both speech and academic subjects—can be frustrating.

Teachers in this field require careful preparation. Teachers need to become familiar with the specialized equipment that is used in auditory training and the specialized skills needed for speech reading and finger spelling. Teachers of hearing-impaired students must also learn how to demonstrate the sounds that make up our spoken language. Teachers in this area must develop strategies to motivate students who feel overwhelmed by the challenges that they face. In addition to these skills, teachers of students who are hearing impaired must develop strong academic skills, and they must bring a sense of optimism and enthusiasm to their work.

People who are interested in a career in this field must earn a B.S. degree in the teaching of hearing-impaired students. Because of the specialized nature of this field, many states and provinces require a master's degree before a prospective teacher can earn a teaching certificate. In addition to their course work, all prospective teachers of hearing-impaired students must complete a supervised teaching experience to earn their teaching certificates.

Opportunities for teachers of students who are hearing impaired should remain steady through the end of this century, with most job openings created by the need to replace retiring teachers.

ACTIVITY AIDE

Suzanne Ward is an activity aide at Clearbrook Center in Rolling Meadows, Illinois.

What made you interested in working with students who are disabled?

I got interested in working at Clearbrook through my sister. She worked as an aide when she was in high school. At first I only took the job because it was close. I needed a job that I could walk to. But now I really like what I do, and I want to go to school to earn a degree in special education.

Would you recommend a career in special education to someone you care about?

It's really hard work. You have to be very patient, and sometimes there is a lot of heavy lifting. It's not for everybody. You have to remember that these people need help.

How would you describe a typical day as an activity aide? What kind of activities tend to dominate your day?

I work on weekends, and I am responsible for a small group of ladies. I lead them in exercises, I help them if they need to go to the bathroom. I help them with classes and activities. I hear people compare it to babysitting sometimes, but it's a lot harder.

What do you view as the most challenging part of your job?

When everyone seems to need my attention at once. My ladies don't understand that I can only do so much at one time.

If you could change one part of your job, what would it be?

The personal care stuff. It's so hard to help people use the bathroom and get themselves dressed.

What do you view as the most rewarding part of your job?

I like my ladies. They take a lot of work, but they're always so happy to see me. It's nice to be able to help people who need help.

If you could give anyone some advice about this field, what would it be?

You need to remember that your people aren't doing anything on purpose. They don't mean to make your job hard, they're just doing the best they can. You've got to be very patient. You've got to repeat things a lot of times. You've got to remember that they're people, and they need to know that you like them and that you care about them.

One of the drawbacks of a career in special education is that people who are interested in this field need to spend years of time and tens of thousands of dollars on an education to prepare them to work with the disabled before they have a real chance to find out if this is the right career for them. One important opportunity for people who think that they might be interested in this field is to work as an aide in a school or in a residential facility.

Aides work directly with people who are disabled in a wide variety of roles. Classroom aides help students stay on track and act as a resource for students who have few academic skills. Activity aides work with those who need help mastering the different steps of activities that are designed to help them develop their fine-motor skills and hand-eye coordination. Aides in residential facilities help people who are disabled with grooming and personal care skills. Most people who are drawn to this field have a strong need to help people who cannot help themselves.

The primary advantage of working as an aide is to learn about those with special needs and how to help them. The experience of working in a school or special education facility can help you decide whether special education should be your life's work. Working as an aide also will allow you to watch professionals at work and to learn from them. The salary range for aides ranges widely, from minimum wage to more than ten dollars an hour. Aides who work full time may have a benefit package that includes insurance, paid holidays, sick time, and vacations. Benefit packages, like salaries, will vary depending on the place of employment.

The minimum educational qualification for most aides is a high school diploma. Aides who work in public or private schools may be required to have some college-level course work. In many cases, people who hold teaching certificates will work as an aide in order to gain experience while they continue to look for full-time teaching work. Many employers will develop their own training programs for aides in order to ensure a consistent level of care for their clients, so aides may be expected to complete a course of study on the job.

The primary disadvantage of working as an aide is that it is a very demanding job, and compared to the salaries paid to certified staff, it does not pay very well. Aides work directly with people with disabilities, and they share the same emotional drains and frustrations that teachers, social workers, physical therapists, and other professionals do. However, because they do not have the appropriate certification and experience, aides make significantly less money. Aides who work in institutions that have no clear guidelines or job descriptions for them may find themselves receiving conflicting directions from many different people.

Because of the relatively high turnover in aide positions, there are usually many opportunities for employment, and as the numbers of those with disabilities increase, the demand for aides is projected to continue to grow.

TEACHER OF STUDENTS WHO ARE PHYSICALLY DISABLED

Bob Carroll is a teacher of students who are physically disabled at Palatine High School in Palatine, Illinois.

What made you interested in helping children with physical disabilities?

I always wanted to be a teacher, but I didn't specialize until college. I had always been interested in working with people who were challenged, and when I did my practice teaching, I chose to work with physically challenged students.

Would you recommend a career in this area to someone you care about?

No question. The only reservation that I might have is in the area of economic concerns. Inclusion and other educational developments might create huge changes in the way that we deliver services.

How would you describe a typical day as a teacher of students with physical disabilities? What kinds of activities tend to dominate your day?

I spend most of my day working with the teaching assistants who work directly with students. Teaching assistants set up lunches, open lockers, take notes, help with bathrooms, and perform many other services for physically challenged students. It is important to schedule teaching assistants carefully and to try to work with individual strengths and weaknesses.

What do you view as the most challenging part of your job?

The most challenging thing I do is to work with students and help them relate to people their own age. This requires a lot of work outside the school day. I try to "sell" school activities to kids and their parents and try to arrange transportation for challenged kids.

What do you view as the most rewarding part of your job?

I work with the same groups of kids for five years at a time. I really enjoy the long-term relationships that develop. It is always gratifying to see former students graduate and lead very productive, happy lives.

If you could give a piece of advice to someone who is about to enter this field, what would it be?

In order to become a successful teacher in this field, you need to get as much experience as you can. Work with challenged people in park district programs, as part of high school work-study, or in recreation programs. Even a good college education is no substitute for hands-on experience.

The United States Department of Education estimates that there are more than 200,000 children in this country who need special education services because they have physical handicaps that make it impossible for them to attend classes in a main-streamed school. Teachers who work with students who are physically handicapped focus on the goal of helping their students develop the self help, daily living, academic, and interpersonal skills they need to become independent human beings.

Teachers of the physically handicapped work as members of an assessment team along with medical personnel, physical therapists, occupational therapists, speech therapists, and social workers. The assessment team evaluates the student's self help skills, trying to determine what activities the student can perform, what kinds of activities might be within the student's range of capability, and what progress the student is making towards these goals. The student's physical mobility and need for physical accommodation are also considered by the assessment team. One important consideration for the team is the student's level, speed, and clarity of communication.

Once the assessment team has completed its work, the special education teacher begins the complicated process of analyzing tasks that students need to learn and developing a sequence of activities that meet these goals. Daily living goals might include activities like feeding and dressing oneself, writing responses or using keyboards to communicate, and using prosthetic devices. In addition to these challenges, special education teachers must teach academic subjects so that physically handicapped students who have normal or above normal intelligence can continue their educations.

Teachers are attracted to this field because they enjoy working with a wide range of intelligence and capabilities in a classroom, and they are committed to the belief that all students need an opportunity to learn and grow. Special education teachers who work with students who are physically handicapped normally work a ten-month school year, and they enjoy the same school holidays that mainstream teachers do. Teachers of physically handicapped students may work in special education cooperatives, or they may work in mainstreamed schools either as a classroom teacher or as a consultant who supervises inclusion aides in several different classrooms or in several different schools. The national average salary for teachers of students who are physically handicapped is $34,000, although salary levels may vary widely from one school district to another.

Teachers who work in this field caution that working with students who are physically handicapped can be very demanding work. It can be very difficult to maintain a positive, optimistic attitude when working with children who are laboring under severe handicaps. Teachers also may feel frustration because students are removed from class and hospitalized for extensive periods of time. Teaching these students requires very close contact with families, and dysfunctional families can undermine progress that the student makes at school. Teachers in this field also warn that there are significant demands on their time because of meetings, staffings, and individualized education programs, too.

In order to become a successful teacher of students who are physically handicapped, teachers need to develop the physical stamina to carry and position students who may not be mobile. Special education teachers need to be positive and optimistic. They need the ability to set clear goals and articulate those goals to their students and to their students' families. Special education teachers must be extremely organized and willing to develop individual education plans for each one of their students.

In order to prepare for this career, prospective teachers must earn a bachelor's degree from an accredited university that offers a program in teaching the physically handicapped. In many areas, teachers also must earn a master's degree in special education before they can be considered for employment. As part of their education, prospective teachers must complete a nine- to eighteen-student teaching experience. As teaching professionals, teachers must be licensed by the state or province in which they teach.

The United States Department of Labor predicts that the demand for teachers of the physically handicapped will remain steady, reflecting the medical advances that allow seriously injured or ill young people to attend school. The movement to include students with handicaps in mainstream schools also will create opportunities for special education teachers.

SPEECH THERAPIST

Phil Breiding is a speech therapist in High School District 214 in the northwest suburbs of Chicago.

What interests or experiences did you have that led you into the field of speech therapy?

I have always had a general interest in speech communication.

Would you recommend a career in this field to someone you care about?

Yes, with some reservations. There are several areas of the helping professions that a person should explore before committing to a specific program.

What facet of your education or work experience helped you to become a successful and effective speech clinician?

I worked in a summer program for handicapped children. That made a tremendous impact on me.

How would you describe a typical day at work? What activities tend to consume most of your time?

Seeing students scheduled for regular therapy sessions, testing students as part of comprehensive case studies and re-evaluations, and the required paperwork.

What is the most rewarding part of your job?

Working with students and seeing improvement in their communication skills.

What is the most frustrating part of your job?

Working with students who don't show up for their appointments.

If you could give a piece of advice to someone who is about to enter this field, what would it be?

Explore the various work settings, such as hospitals and clinics as well as schools. Don't just focus on public schools.

Most of us think of speech as a natural, effortless activity, but millions of people are handicapped by their inability to speak clearly. This handicap takes many forms: it may involve stuttering, an inability to form the beginning and ending sounds of words, or a problem with speech and language development.

Speech therapists who work with school districts deal with all of these problems as they help students learn to communicate. Speech therapists diagnose speech disorders and develop treatment plans for their students. School speech therapists spend much of their time screening students to see if they need help and then providing direct service for those students. As part of the treatment plan, speech therapists may need to communicate with parents, teachers, and the school psychologist. Speech therapists provide important information about students who are being recommended for special education services, and they are frequently called on to participate in staffings.

People who are drawn to speech therapy want to help people communicate. At times speech therapists make dramatic progress—students who were virtual outcasts in school learn to communicate, establish friendships, share ideas, and develop a sense of belonging and community at school. At other times, progress may be painfully slow. Speech therapists who work for school districts usually work out of clean, comfortable offices. They have the opportunity to be part of the life of a school, enjoying the excitement and high energy levels of a school and working the same hours and days as members of the teaching staff. Speech therapists may use the extra time afforded by typical school holidays to develop their own private practice or to spend time with friends and family. In many school districts, speech therapists are paid on the same salary schedule as teachers, so salary levels may vary from one school district to another. The national average for speech therapists is between $25,000 and $38,000 a year.

Because of the constant practice and repetition involved, speech therapy requires intense concentration and tremendous patience. Progress is often measured in tiny increments. Speech therapists also are required to keep detailed records, describing the diagnosis, treatment plan, and progress of each student. Given a heavy caseload and the competing demands for meetings, screenings, and paperwork, speech therapists can be very stressed by their jobs.

Many speech therapists travel between two or more schools, which only adds to the burden of their job. Other frustrations can develop over parent support, client attendance, and conflict over treatment plans. Certainly the most difficult issue for anyone in the helping professions is the realization that it is impossible to help everyone. The depth of the handicap, the family support systems, and the student's willingness to cooperate may undermine the most carefully developed treatment plans.

Because speech therapists often deal with very subtle shadings of sound, people who are interested in this field need excellent listening skills and the ability to concentrate for long periods of time. Potential therapists also need to develop strong organizational skills, make the most of their limited time, and keep accurate records. As members of one of the helping professions, speech therapists need a combination of warmth, empathy, and optimism that is balanced by objectivity and honesty. Speech therapists need to be able to diagnose problems and work on solutions. They must have the ability to develop plans, listen for feedback, and adapt their plans to meet their client's needs. The process of planning and adapting requires genuine skill in problem solving.

Communication skills are critical to successful speech therapists as so much of their time is spent working with individuals. Speech therapists need to be able to discuss problems and goals clearly, and they must be able to communicate with parents, teachers, administrators, and students.

In order to become a speech therapist, students need a bachelor's degree in speech and a master's degree in speech pathology. Besides the course work involved in earning these degrees, students must spend three hundred hours of their time in a supervised clinical setting, such as a hospital, clinic, or school. In order to become a licensed speech therapist, students in the United States and Canada must take and pass a national examination and complete a nine-month internship.

There are about 34,000 speech therapists at work right now. The United States Department of Labor predicts that the demand for additional therapists should grow both in schools and in the private sector due to expanding need for service and the need to replace therapists who are retiring.

TEACHER OF STUDENTS WHO ARE
VISUALLY HANDICAPPED

Denise Clouser is a teacher of students who are visually handicapped at the Low Incidence Program in the northwest suburbs of Chicago.

What made you interested in working with students who are visually handicapped?

I worked with visually impaired students when I was a student assistant in high school. It was a wonderful experience, and I decided that I wanted to spend my career working with visually impaired students.

Would you recommend a career in this area to someone you care about?

Yes. I really enjoy this work. It is challenging work, but it is very worthwhile.

How would you describe a typical day as a teacher of students who are visually handicapped? What kinds of activities tend to dominate your day?

I work with individual students on a one-to-one basis. I teach students to become mobile in the school and in the community.

What do you view as the most challenging part of your job?

Teachers who work with visually impaired students often work with a wide range of ages, from preschool to high school. Many visually impaired students also have other disabilities that impede their progress.

What do you view as the most rewarding part of your job?

I really enjoy the interaction with kids. I enjoy watching them succeed. In special programs we tend to work with the same groups of kids for a long period of time, and we develop nice relationships. It's a pleasure to watch these young people grow up.

Most of the traditional tools that teachers use are visual: the blackboard, the overhead projector, textbooks, movies or video-tapes. Teachers who work with students who are visually handicapped do not have access to any of these tools. Teachers of the visually impaired need to help their students develop listening skills that enable them to succeed in school and in adult life. They also need to help these students develop the academic skills that will prepare them for advanced study or for a vocation.

Teachers of students who are visually impaired usually work with small groups of students in mainstream elementary or high schools. These teachers use special tools such as computers, Braille keyboards, and the Kurzweil reading machine to present ideas to students. The ultimate goal of these teachers is to integrate their students into mainstream classrooms. One primary responsibility of teachers in this field is to develop or adapt instructional materials for visually impaired students. Special education teachers must develop an individualized education program for each student, and they must keep careful records about each student's progress towards educational or social goals. Although classes for visually impaired students are small, teachers need to help students with a wide range of educational skills and needs.

Teachers who work with students who are visually impaired enjoy the challenge of helping young people overcome their handicaps. These teachers also enjoy working with small groups of students. Although the work is very demanding, teachers can look forward to many school holidays, which allow time for professional or personal growth. The national average salary for teachers in this field is $34,000, but salaries tend to depend on an individual teacher's level of education and years of experience. Individual school districts and special education cooperatives also have salary schedules that vary widely.

The main difficulty that practitioners of this field discuss is the difficulty of preparing individualized educational plans for each student and the record keeping that those plans entail. A second area of concern is the need to work with students who have a wide range of skills and needs. Certainly teachers who enter this field must be able to organize their time well. Teachers of students who are visually impaired must develop strong communication skills and the ability to discuss abstract ideas without relying on traditional, vision-based classroom aids. Perhaps the most important quality that teachers in this field need is the ability to believe that visually impaired students can learn and achieve in spite of their disabilities. As with all teachers, successful teachers of visually impaired students must combine enthusiasm for their subject areas with concern and care for their students.

It takes a great deal of training to become a teacher of students who are visually impaired. People who are interested in this field often major in education as undergraduates and specialize in the education of the visually impaired in graduate school. All states and provinces require teachers to be licensed, and in many areas, prospective teachers must pass a certifying examination before they can be licensed to teach.

Because students who are visually impaired make up a small portion of the student population, there are only a limited number of teaching jobs available for people who want to work with the visually impaired. The demand for teachers will remain low, with most teaching jobs developing as school districts and special education cooperatives replace teachers who retire.

OCCUPATIONAL THERAPIST

Dianna Newman is an occupational therapist at Palatine High School in Palatine, Illinois.

What interests or experiences led you into the field of occupational therapy?

I worked in a children's nursing home when I was in high school, and I worked under the supervision of an occupational therapist. I was very interested in this field.

Would you recommend a career in occupational therapy to someone you care about?

This is an excellent career for someone who is interested in working with people.

How would you describe a typical workday? What kinds of activities tend to dominate your day?

I work with students on upper-extremity exercises. I spend a lot of time with students teaching them to use the keyboard and computer so they can work on memory and cognitive skills as well as fine motor coordination.

What do you view as the most challenging part of your job?

Helping young people who have many disabilities in addition to their primary disability. I spend a lot of time working on problem-solving skills and on establishing focus.

If you could give a piece of advice to someone who is about to enter this field, what would it be?

Spend time doing volunteer work in any type of health-care facility. The time you spend working in health care will give you a perspective on the rewards and challenges in this field.

Occupational therapists work with patients to help them participate as fully as possible in regular school activities. Occupational therapists focus on motor and reasoning skills. They evaluate individual clients and design an individualized program for each one. Individualized treatment programs might include training for hand/eye coordination and visual discrimination and training on intellectual skills, such as problem solving, decision making, memory, and perception. Occupational therapists also may work with clients to teach them how to use specially designed adaptive equipment, such as wheelchairs or aids for such activities as dressing and eating. In many areas occupational therapists lead support groups for people who are adjusting to their handicaps.

Although much of their work day is spent in direct service to their clients, occupational therapists also must make time for staff meetings. Therapists who work for school districts or special education cooperatives must make time for parent meetings and staffings. All occupational therapists must budget time for maintaining accurate and detailed records for each client's treatment and progress.

People who are drawn to this field enjoy working with people who need help. Although the work can be physically exhausting as well as emotionally draining, occupational therapists can make a positive impact on the lives of people who need help. As professionals, occupational therapists have a great deal of control over their own schedules and work with minimal direct supervision. The national average salary for occupational therapists is $34,000 a year, although therapists who are paid on a school district's salary schedule may earn significantly more. Occupational therapists who work in school systems also benefit from a ten-month school year and from frequent school holidays. These holidays allow therapists enough time to develop private practices or to devote time to family life or professional growth.

All careers have some drawbacks, and people who work in this field often feel frustrated by their inability to help every client. Individual clients may pose problems by failing to cooperate on treatment plans, and at times treatment plans may not work. The pressure of working with seriously ill or injured young people can also be very draining. In many school districts, occupational therapists feel that their caseloads are becoming unmanageable because tight budgets don't allow their programs to expand.

People who are interested in this field need a minimum of four years of training to understand the kinds of illnesses and injuries that their clients may suffer from and to learn appropriate therapies and techniques to treat these problems. Occupational therapists also need to develop the physical stamina that is needed for this job. Successful occupational therapists develop communication skills that allow them to understand what clients are trying to tell them. Occupational therapists need strong communication skills to explain what activities the patients must perform and why these activities are important. People in this field need to be patient, caring, and sympathetic. Occupational therapy requires some very repetitive work as well as contact with people who are living through an extremely difficult time and who may not be very cooperative.

In order to become a licensed occupational therapist, prospective therapists must earn a B.S. degree in occupational therapy from an accredited university. As part of their education, prospective therapists must complete a supervised clinical experience, which usually lasts for about six months. In the United States and Canada, prospective therapists also must pass a national certifying examination.

At the moment, more than 36,000 occupational therapists work in hospitals, schools, and clinics. The department of labor predicts that there will be a moderate increase in the demand for occupational therapists as schools continue to expand services for handicapped students.

CHAPTER 3

CAREERS WITH THE BEHAVIOR DISORDERED

TEACHER OF STUDENTS WITH BEHAVIOR DISORDERS

John Lipniski teaches students with behavior disorders at Amundsen High School in Chicago.

What interests or experiences led you into the field of special education?

I was interested in working with smaller groups of students and working with students who have special needs.

Would you recommend a career in this field to someone you care about?

Yes. Special education can be very rewarding, especially when slow learners become successful.

How would you describe a typical day as a teacher of students with behavior disorders? What kinds of activities tend to dominate your day?

I spend much of my time changing lesson plans to adapt to the daily needs of students. Counseling and individual tutoring dominate my day.

What do you view as the most challenging part of your job?

Adapting to the individual needs of students.

If you could you change one part of your job, what would it be?

Spend less time on the behavioral modification of students.

What do you view as the most rewarding part of your job?

Seeing students graduate from high school.

If you could give a piece of advice to someone who is about to enter this field, what would it be?

Be patient and listen to the students before you try to set up an educational program for them.

One of the most confusing and frustrating issues in special education is the area of behavior disorders. There is no clinical definition of behavior disorders; there are no tests that measure appropriate or inappropriate behaviors. The working definition of behavior disorders describes behaviors that go to an extreme, behaviors that repeatedly break social and cultural expectations.

Behavior disorders are often grouped into internalizing and externalizing behaviors. Externalizing behavior is described as defiance, disobedience, aggression, vandalism, and theft. Internalizing behavior is described as withdrawal, depression, and immaturity. Children who exhibit internalizing behaviors have no friends, won't play with children their own age, and demand help with every activity.

The question of just which children are handicapped by behavior disorders is full of ambiguities. Although all children are shy and withdrawn with some people or in some situations, children with behavior disorders are always withdrawn. And though "normal" children sometimes hit, kick, or bite when they have been provoked, behavior-disordered children become violent or aggressive without provocation.

Children with behavior disorders also are difficult to identify because there does not seem to be any physical reason for their behavior. Children may have learned that aggression will bring status and rewards instead of adverse consequences. Children who exhibit internalizing behavior may have learned that withdrawal is the best way to cope with a hostile environment.

Teachers who work with children with behavior disorders have two full-time jobs: on one hand they have a responsibility to meet their student's academic needs. Teachers of elementary school children are responsible for the full range of academic subjects. Teachers in secondary school teach their own subject areas. On the other hand, though academic growth is important, a larger, more difficult task is to teach these children alternatives to their inappropriate behaviors.

Teachers who choose to work with behavior-disordered children enter this profession because they want to help people who desperately need help. Typically students with behavior disorders have been deeply scarred by their home lives. The teacher that they spend their school day with may be the only caring, mature, emotionally stable adult they see. The school environment may be the safest, most accepting environment they know.

Although special education is hard work, teachers work roughly ten months a year and have frequent school holidays. Salaries vary from on school district to another, but the average salary for teachers who work with behavior-disordered students is $37,500 dollars a year. Teachers with advanced degrees and increased seniority earn more.

The dual nature of teaching in special education creates a lot of stress. All of the students in special education are extremely needy and frequently impulsive. Students with behavior disorders can exhibit behavior that is exasperating and, at times, violent. Relations with the parents of behavior-disordered students also may be a source of difficulty. In many cases children with behavior disorders have parents with behavior disorders themselves. Even though these people may be a substantial cause of their children's problems, they must be included in all of the major decisions that concern their children.

Special education teachers also may be frustrated both by the lack of achievement they see in their students and by the steady flow of paperwork, which includes individualized education plans for each student as well as feedback for parents, school officials, and school health workers. Teachers also invest a great deal of time in staffings and other meetings.

In order to help their students, teachers in this area need strong academic skills, a repertoire of behavior management techniques, and tremendous organizational skills. They need to be able to create individualized education plans for each student, and they must be able to maintain their records on a regular basis. Teachers must be able to face many difficult academic and behavior issues at once. They must be emotionally stable and mature, empathetic and understanding. At the same time they need to be able to set limits and enforce consequences without escalating negative behaviors. Because students with behavior disorders have difficulty expressing themselves, teachers in this field must be skilled in reading facial expressions, body language, and other visual cues to their behavior.

In order to specialize in teaching behavior-disordered students, it is necessary to earn a B.S. degree in education, which will include a nine- to eighteen-week student teaching experience. Because of the close relationship between students with behavior disorders and those with learning disabilities, many school districts in the United States and Canada require certification in both subject areas. All teachers must be licensed by the state or province in which they teach, and in some states, licensing must include a written examination. Salary increases will almost always depend on further education and experience.

The United States Department of Education predicts a steady rise in the number of school-age children throughout the rest of this century and a consequent rise in the number of special education teachers who will be needed to serve them. Although most teaching jobs will be created by the public school system, teachers also will be needed to work in hospitals, private schools, special education cooperatives, and in prisons.

TEACHER OF STUDENTS WITH SEVERE AND PROFOUND BEHAVIOR DISORDERS

Jane Haeger is a teacher of students with behavior disorders at the Behavior Education Center in Wheeling, Illinois.

What interests or events led you into the field of special education?

I knew that I was going to become a teacher when I was in fourth grade. Our teacher was humiliating one of my friends because she couldn't write well. I told myself that I would be a teacher some day, and that I would never treat children that way. I earned a teaching certificate, and then I worked as an aide in special education after I graduated from college. I went back to school at night to become certified to teach in special education.

Would you recommend a career in this field to someone you care about?

Definitely. It is important to realize that this work can be frustrating and challenging. But it is never boring.

How would you describe a typical workday? What kinds of activities tend to dominate your day?

Talking, listening, working with people. In this field it is important to communicate and to listen well. I spend a lot of time problem solving with students who have educational and personal problems. I guess I would describe my day as a constant exchange of communication with kids.

If you could change anything about your job, what would it be?

There is nothing that I would change. The staff at B.E.C. has worked hard to develop materials and behavior modification strategies for our students. We have a good working relationship with our students and with other staff members.

What part of your education or work experience was most valuable in terms of helping you become a successful teacher in this field?

The time I spent working as an aide in special education was invaluable to me. My experience as a parent was very helpful, and my experience working with Girl Scouts taught me some very useful problem-solving skills, as well as activities that help students learn decision-making and leadership skills.

If you could give one piece of advice to someone who is about to enter this field, what would it be?

Work as an aide or paraprofessional before you enter this field. Take advantage of summer school problems or park district programs. If your high school offers credit for on-the-job training, make use of it. On-the-job experience allows you to see whether this will be a good job fit for you.

Most people think of behavior disorders as a question of "being bad," but young people with severe behavior disorders are faced with serious problems. Children with severe behavior disorders may lack the ability to care for themselves, dress themselves, feed themselves, or use the bathroom without help. These young people often do not respond to voices or to visual signals. They may have normal language development, or they may parrot back phrases that they happen to hear. They also may invent a mixture of words and sounds that they use in place of language.

Some students with severe and profound behavior disorders may shut themselves off from everything around them and go into complete withdrawal. Other students may be extremely aggressive. It is not unusual for students with severe behavior disorders to develop self-stimulating behaviors that they repeat incessantly: making noises, twisting objects, or swinging their heads back and forth. In some cases children with severe and profound behavior disorders seem to intentionally hurt themselves but do not appear to feel any pain. In nearly every case, severely disordered students seem to be cut off from the world around them, and they seem to view other people and inanimate objects without feelings or intelligence.

Teachers who choose to work with these very needy young people must focus on changing student behavior, with the goal of preparing young people to work and live as independent human beings. In order to be successful in these goals, teachers need to develop a wide range of behavior modification techniques that will encourage and reward positive changes in student behavior. Teachers who work in this field must be able to diagnose problems and work toward finding solutions. They must be able to work with several students at the same time. People who enter this profession need to be calm, caring, patient, and emotionally stable. They need to set limits, enforce consequences, and reward positive behavior.

Teaching is not a glamorous profession, and working with disabled students can be emotionally and physically exhausting. Teachers who choose this area of concentration will have the satisfaction of knowing that they are helping students who truly need help. Teachers of students with severe and profound behavior disorders typically work ten months a year, with frequent school holidays. The salary range for teachers in this area is from $21,000 to $33,700 a year. However, each special education cooperative and school district established its own salary schedule, so some organizations may pay significantly higher salaries.

This is challenging work. Severely disordered students require a tremendous investment of time and energy. The students must be carefully supervised at all times because of their impulsive and sometimes hostile behavior. Because these are very serious problems, progress can be painfully slow. Dysfunctional family dynamics or conflict away from school can undermine months of patient work.

Perhaps the most frustrating aspect of teaching these students is the sense of isolation that teachers feel. Teachers have very limited contact with other adults during the day, and the nature of the disability dictates that the student will view the teacher as an object, without empathy or concern.

Teachers who choose this profession will need a wide range of behavior modification skills and strong organizational skills to prepare the different activities required by such individualized education needs. Effective teachers need to be able to assess feedback from students and select the correct approach for each child. Teachers who are successful in this field are empathetic, calm, caring people who can set limits and provide consequences for inappropriate behavior. They must also have the ability to develop and provide rewards for appropriate behavior.

These skills take time to develop. Prospective teachers must earn a bachelor's degree in education with a special emphasis in behavior disorders. As part of their education, they must complete a student teaching experience. All teachers are licensed, and many states and provinces require competency testing as part of the licensing process. Although individual school districts and special education cooperatives will hire according to local school enrollments and budgets, in general the demand for teachers of severe and profound behavior disordered students will continue to grow, reflecting the general growth in school enrollments that will continue through the rest of the 1990s.

CHAPTER 4

CAREERS WITH THE MENTALLY IMPAIRED

TEACHER OF STUDENTS WHO ARE MILDLY MENTALLY IMPAIRED

Laura Koenig is a teacher of the Young Adult Program in Rolling Meadows, Illinois.

What interests or experiences led you into the field of special education?

I always wanted to teach, and I always wanted to help people.

Would you recommend a career in special education to someone you care about?

Yes, if they have the patience and commitment to work with young people.

How would you describe a typical workday? What kind of activities tend to dominate your day?

Most of the work is fairly repetitive. We work on mastering skills, and we spend a lot of time on learning how to learn.

What do you view as the most challenging part of your job?

The students sometimes become very frustrated with their lack of progress. Sometimes behavior issues get in the way of learning.

If you could change one part of your job, what would it be?

I would want to work with smaller classes.

What do you view as the most rewarding part of your job?

Helping students master skills and work toward mainstreaming.

If you could give advice to someone who is about to enter this field, what would it be?

Realize that this is not a glamorous job, but it is a very important one. It is important to get hands-on experience as early as possible to know that you are making the right career move.

Teachers who work with students who are mildly mentally impaired develop individualized education plans that are designed to help students learn life skills, social skills, and academic skills. A teacher of mildly mentally impaired students will have the ultimate goal of preparing students to become self-supporting, independent adults. For example, a teacher developing units on life skills would teach the step-by-step process of following a recipe, running a vacuum cleaner, making change, or handling money.

Children who are mentally impaired often have a great deal of difficulty interpreting social cues, so teachers focus on social skills to improve their students' abilities to develop a satisfying social life and to feel comfortable in situations with mainstream students. Teachers who work with students who are mentally impaired try to develop enough academic skills to prepare students for vocational training. In developing these skills, the teachers will need to help their students overcome problems with attention, memory, and problem solving. Students who are mildly mentally impaired are bombarded with visual and sound cues, and they have trouble deciding just which cues they need to attend to. This problem is compounded by short attention spans and difficulty remembering information. Multistep problems pose special challenges because some children may not be able to remember the steps or the sequence of steps involved in solving the problem.

One of the most heartbreaking behaviors that teachers who work with these students encounter is the "pencil down syndrome," in which students become so overwhelmed by a problem or assignment that they simply stop working. They don't move on to another problem or ask for help; they just give up. Teachers who work with students who are mildly mentally impaired must be willing to give frequent reassurance and reinforcement to their students, so these students can overcome the sense of helplessness in the face of difficult work.

Although the work is challenging, teachers in this field have the opportunity to help young people reach their greatest potential. Whether they work in public or private schools, teachers in this area generally work a ten-month school year. This schedule allows a long block of time that can be spent on personal or professional growth activities, such as additional schooling. Or, the time can be used with family or friends. Public school salaries vary from one school district to another but average between $20,000 and $40,000 a year. Typically, salary increases depend on length of service and advanced education.

Teachers who enter this field must be willing to accept the challenge of preparing individual education plans for each one of their students. They must address behavior problems and problems with motivation, as well as the student's academic needs. The preparation and maintenance of individual education plans is a tremendous burden. Teachers may feel frustrated by the amount of time that they must spend in meetings and by the amount of time that is spent repeating information. Individual students may go through cycles of academic and emotional growth and regression that can be very difficult to deal with.

Teachers who work with students who are mildly mentally impaired must learn how to break ideas and activities into smaller units that can be learned one step at a time. These students can learn complex activities, but only if they have the opportunity to master one portion of the activity at a time. Teachers must also learn appropriate problem-solving skills, so when their students are faced with a decision, they can develop a menu of options and employ a decision-making strategy.

Teachers who choose this career must be patient and compassionate. Because they work in a fairly high stress job, it is important that they be emotionally stable and responsible. Teachers must be willing to develop strategies to motivate students who do not always respond to traditional motivators, such as grades, and who have very limited support for any school activity when they get home. In order to learn the skills they need, teachers must complete a four-year degree program from an accredited university and major in the field of special education. Prospective teachers also must complete a successful student teaching experience. Many states require that prospective teachers pass a state or provincial licensing examination before they can be licensed to teach.

Currently there are more than 332,000 teachers working in special education. The United States Department of Labor estimates that this number will continue to grow as more MMI students enter mainstream schools and as an aging teaching population retires.

TEACHER OF STUDENTS WHO ARE SEVERELY MENTALLY HANDICAPPED

Patricia Givens is a teacher of students who are severely mentally handicapped at the Kirk Center in Palatine, Illinois.

What made you interested in helping children who are severely mentally handicapped?

I got hooked on the kids' personalities. Many people in special education say that we learn more from the kids than they learn from us. I think it's true. These kids have some insights into human behavior that are really meaningful. They can really teach us about life.

Would you recommend a career in this area to someone you care about?

Yes, but you must be willing to prepare for this career, and you need to have some hands-on experience so you know that this is the right career for you.

How would you describe a typical day as a teacher of children who are severely mentally handicapped? What kinds of activities tend to dominate your day?

I spend my time trying to help students become more independent, so they can care for themselves. We work on self-care skills, such as toileting, feeding, hygiene, and grooming.

What do you view as the most challenging part of your job?

The hardest part of my job is the problem of dealing consistently, empathetically, and fairly with students when they act out. It is very important to try to understand why children act out. Sometimes the causes are related to development or sensory stimulation. Sometimes it is a question of "terrible twos." Students need help in dealing with their rage issues.

What do you view as the most rewarding part of your job?

Helping students alleviate their behavior problems.

If you could give a piece of advice to someone who is about to enter this field, what would it be?

You need hands-on experience in order to know whether this is the right career for you. Work in a summer school program, a park district program, or look for an opportunity to do work-study. Many people are put off by the daily care demands of this job; other people really get hooked by the understanding and acceptance of these kids.

Teachers who work with students who are severely mentally handicapped focus on developing their life skills, with the goal of helping their charges develop the skills that will allow them a measure of independent life. These life skills include grooming, bathing, toileting, dressing, and such domestic skills as cooking, cleaning, shopping, and leisure activities.

On the surface, this would not appear to be a very demanding curriculum, but life skills, like academic skills, involve mastering a complex sequence of steps. In order to help their students learn these steps, special education teachers need to assess skills and develop individual instructional plans that will allow their students to meet their goals. One important strategy that special education teachers use is to develop simulations that will allow their students to practice the separate steps in a multistep project, such as shopping, making change, ordering food at a restaurant, or trying to communicate. As many students who are severely mentally handicapped have a great deal of difficulty recognizing and interpreting social cues, special education teachers must find and reinforce prompts for appropriate verbal and nonverbal communication.

Working with severely handicapped children is very rewarding work. People who enter this area of specialization derive great satisfaction from helping young people begin to gain some control over their lives. Special education teachers generally work a ten-month school year and enjoy frequent school holidays. As working professionals, special education teachers have the opportunity to develop their own classroom schedule, and they have very little day-to-day supervision. Although salary levels vary from one school district to another, the national average is $34,000.

Professionals who choose to work with students who are severely handicapped sometimes feel overwhelmed by the challenges of developing individual education plans for each one of their students. Some professionals are frustrated by the difficulty of working with parents and other family members. Many severely handicapped students go through cycles of progress and regression that can be very stressing.

In order to be an effective teacher of students who are severely mentally handicapped, prospective teachers need to be extremely organized and must develop the skills to be able to work with several people at the same time. Successful teachers are able to create a safe, predictable environment for their students. Successful teachers set limits and enforce them. Teachers of severely mentally handicapped students must be patient, optimistic, and nurturing, even in the face of repeated setbacks.

In order to qualify for a career in this area, prospective teachers must earn a bachelor's degree in the teaching of mentally handicapped students from an accredited university. Many states and provinces require a master's degree as the minimum requirement for a teaching certificate. All teachers must complete a nine- to eighteen-week teacher training program before they can be licensed.

The demand for teachers of students who are severely mentally handicapped will remain steady throughout the rest of the century, with most teaching positions developing as the result of retirements.

CHAPTER 5

OTHER SPECIAL EDUCATION CAREERS

SCHOOL NURSE

Joanne Patano is a school nurse at Rolling Meadows High School in Rolling Meadows, Illinois.

What made you decide to become a school nurse?

I thoroughly enjoy working with teens and their families. I used to work as the head nurse of family planning in ob/gyn clinics in Chicago where the median age for clients was fifteen years old.

Would you recommend a career in school nursing to someone you care about?

Yes, because if that individual was kind, caring, and dynamic, he or she could make a difference in a young person's life.

What academic experience or work experience was most valuable in helping you become a successful and effective school nurse?

My school nurse internship, as well as the experience of subbing for a variety of school districts.

What kind of impact has the epidemic of sexually transmitted diseases had on school nursing?

I see many students for this very problem, but it is not new, and I did expect it. My experience as head nurse in a family planning clinic helped me understand what to expect and to develop a referral base.

How would you describe a typical workday? What kinds of activities tend to dominate your day?

I love it! There is no "typical" day. Every day is exciting, challenging, and is fast paced because of crisis intervention and counseling that goes along with my job.

What is the most rewarding part of your job?

Touching a student's life and making a difference. I just received a letter from a student who is now attending college, and I realized just how much of a difference I made in her life.

If you could change any part of your job, what would it be?

I would change the layout of the office to provide more privacy for kids, so I could do assessments and discuss them in private. Clerical help would be a pleasure—a dream!

If you could give a piece of advice to someone who is about to enter the field of school nursing, what would it be?

You have to love kids, you have to set limits effectively, you have to love change, and you have to be a team member!

A school nurse serves as the health and wellness leader for the entire school community. The school nurse deals with medical emergencies and provides leadership in teaching students about the dangers of alcohol and drug abuse and the dangers of sexually transmitted diseases. School nurses take an active role in crisis situations at school, and they involve state and local welfare agencies when students need them. The school nurse is also responsible for maintaining health and immunization records for the student population.

A school nurse is expected to communicate with students and parents and is responsible for informing teachers when their students may have a medical issue that requires special consideration from them. The school nurse participates in staff meetings and screenings when there may be questions about a student's health.

School nurses take a leadership role in promoting wellness throughout the school community by developing programs on nutrition, exercise, and choices that promote a healthy lifestyle.

When asked why they like their jobs, school nurses talk about the pleasure of working with kids and the sense of accomplishment they feel when they have made a difference in a young person's life. School nurses usually work out of a clean, well-organized office. As health care professionals, school nurses decide what activities need to be done each workday. They have minimal day-to-day supervision, and they are free to deal with emergencies or set goals for themselves. Although a school nurse may have a very heavy workload, it is never boring or routine. School nurses are often paid on the same salary schedule as the teachers in a school district, so salary levels will vary throughout the country. On the average, salaries for nurses range from $23,000 to $50,000 a year. School nurses work during school hours and have the same vacations and holidays as members of the teaching staff, a schedule that allows time for family commitments and professional growth.

School nursing is a very challenging career. Perhaps the greatest challenge that nurses face is the perception that a school nurse is a woman in a starched white cap who sits in her office waiting for the chance to put a bandage on a bruised finger. School nurses help students with serious emotional and physical problems every day. They deal with the frustration of working with parents who may refuse to acknowledge their child's need for help. In some cases, law enforcement and state welfare officials may not be able to provide the assistance that a student needs. A caseload that combines crisis intervention and detailed examination of student health records can be stressing. School nurses who have to travel between schools may feel that there is simply not enough time in the workday too keep up with student needs. An additional source of frustration is the absence of any kind of career ladder. Once hired, school nurses tend to keep the same job description for as long as they keep their jobs.

People who enter this profession need strong communication skills. They must be able to relate to young people and to adults. This field demands an ability to handle pressure and stress. A successful school nurse must develop excellent problem-solving skills. Certainly one of the most important skills that a school nurse needs to develop is the ability to pay careful attention to detail. Medications, immunization records, and health histories all require meticulous attention to detail.

In order to become a school nurse, students first must become registered nurses. This requires that students complete a four-year college program and earn a bachelor's degree in nursing. Many colleges offer teacher-nurse certification, which provides extra insight into the special problems of becoming a school nurse. Teacher-nurse certification is not always required in order to become a school nurse, but it is extremely helpful and may be an important factor in obtaining a school nursing job.

At the moment, there is a persistent shortage of registered nurses, but there is usually a good deal of competition for school nursing positions. Applicants with teacher nurse certification or with public health experience may have a real advantage in job placement.

TEACHER OF STUDENTS WHO ARE
LEARNING DISABLED

Susan Andrich Horan is a high school LD teacher at Rolling Meadows High School in Rolling Meadows, Illinois.

What made you decide to go into this field of special education?

I worked with mildly retarded kids when I was young.

Would you recommend this field to someone you care about?

Yes.

Was there a particular class or work experience that prepared you to become a successful, effective teacher?

No. I learned mainly through experience. Many ongoing workshops and classes have given me ideas and strategies to try.

If you were asked to give new teachers in special education some advice, what would it be?

Make sure that you know the students' behavioral intellect when you start to work with them. This takes much patience, constant reteaching, and lots of different teaching strategies.

How would you describe a typical day as a special education teacher?

Every day is a little different. Basically though, we have five classes like everyone else. We are team teaching, and we have to relate to lots of different teachers and parents.

What is the most rewarding part of your job?

Watching kids grow and actually understand concepts.

What is the most frustrating part of your job?

Kids not retaining the information that you just taught.

The United States Department of Education estimates that 5 percent of all school-aged children have some kind of learning disability. These are students with average or above average intelligence who don't seem to be able to pay attention in class, remember or process information, or solve problems on their own.

Aside from problems with low achievement in school, these young people also may be hyperactive—seemingly unable to control themselves and sit at a desk. The students may have trouble with physical coordination and have emotional problems, such as sudden changes in mood and an inability to control impulsive behavior.

Teachers who work with students with learning disabilities must have strong academic skills, and they must develop individualized education programs in order to help each student deal with this disability. One of the most important part of the LD teacher's job is to help students develop strategies to approach their schoolwork, to decide what an assignment really asks for, and to develop a plan to do one part of an activity or assignment at a time. Students with learning disabilities need help developing problem-solving skills. Frequently they feel trapped by situations and choose the one option that comes to mind, instead of defining a problem, reviewing the options, and making an informed choice. In order to perform well at school, these students need to work on techniques that help them memorize information and allow them to build self-checking skills. This way they can check to see if they actually understand the material that they hear or read, or if they are simply hearing sounds or glancing at words.

Teachers who work with students with learning disabilities must develop strategies that help students acquire these important skills. Students with learning disabilities tend to have very poor self concepts and have difficulty getting along with their peers. Psychologists argue that this problem comes from misdirected social cues. Learning-disabled students are inclined to misinterpret comments, gestures, and feelings, and this can lead to painful social situations. Poor problem-solving skills and an inability to look at situations from another person's perspective complicate this problem.

One of the greatest challenges LD teachers face is the need to develop individualized education programs to remediate the learned helplessness that seems to characterize these students. Students sometimes feel as though they have no control over their own lives. They do not seem to be able to make decisions or assume any sense of self direction. These young people are often described as "drifting" through their own lives.

Although teaching can be very difficult work, it can be deeply rewarding. When students with learning disabilities acquire the skills they need, they can make dramatic progress in school. More important still, they can develop friendships and enjoy a rewarding social life. Most LD teachers work in regular education or mainstreamed schools, and they enjoy the social life that a school can offer. Special education teachers also work the same hours as the other members of the teaching staff and enjoy the same school holidays and extended summer vacation. This schedule allows time not only for family and friends, but time for continued professional growth. Although salaries vary from one school district to another, the national average falls between $30,000 and $40,000 a year. More affluent school districts can pay significantly higher salaries.

The greatest disadvantage of teaching students with learning disabilities is the constant need to deal with both academic concerns and behavior issues at the same time. Teachers also are frustrated by tremendous amounts of paperwork in the form of individualized education plans for each student. In addition, LD teachers must devote time to meetings, staffings, and yearly reviews of each students. Teachers who are interested in working with these students need to learn behavior modification techniques, and they need to learn many different strategies for teaching students, such as process training, multisensory approaches, cognitive training, and direct instruction. Teachers who work in this field must be patient and empathetic. They must be able to set limits and enforce consequences, but they must be able to do this without escalating a situation until it provokes hostile or violent behavior. It is important that teachers in this field view academic concerns and behavior issues as problems to be solved, not as personal attacks.

In order to become an LD teacher, it is necessary to earn a B.S. degree from an accredited university and major in education with an emphasis on teaching students with learning disabilities. Because there is a close relationship between students with learning disabilities and those with behavior disorders, many school districts in the United States and Canada require certification in both areas. Before graduating, all prospective LD teachers must complete a student teaching experience. All LD teachers are certified by the state or province that they teach in, and this certification process may include competency testing.

As student enrollments continue to grow throughout the end of this century, opportunities for LD teachers also will grow. Teachers will be needed to serve students who are identified as being in need of help, and teachers will be needed to replace an aging workforce. Job growth in individual school districts will depend on school finances and enrollments.

SPECIAL EDUCATION SUPERVISOR

Sam De Falco is the director of the Individual Resources Program at Rolling Meadows High School in Rolling Meadows, Illinois.

What interests or experiences led you into the field of special education?

My college training was in counselor education, so I was always interested in helping. Kids with little or no school success seemed to need the most help.

Would you recommend a career in special education to someone you care about?

Yes, with the provision that field work, or observation, occur early on in one's training to validate one's interests and to help determine which disability one is most interested in, such as learning disability, hearing impaired, blind, physically disabled, or any one of many other specializations.

How would you describe a typical day as an individual resources coordinator? What kinds of activities tend to dominate your day?

My job involves helping to verify the effectiveness of students' special education programs. We need to adjust our teaching, our resources, our efforts to meet students' needs. This process always involves parents. School meetings, I.E.P. conferences, meetings with counselors and teachers dominate my workday.

What is the most challenging part of your job?

The most challenging part of my job involves the continuing need to help staff understand the ways in which schools need to adapt to meet the needs of individual students, especially severely and profoundly disabled students.

If you could change one part of your job, what would it be?

I wish that teachers from different divisions would work more collaboratively toward helping students succeed. Too much time is spent by too many people in identifying problems and looking for other people or teachers or deans to handle them.

What is the most rewarding part of your job?

Being able to make room for all students at the Rolling Meadows High School "table." Schools need to be open to all students in a community. Special schools that only work with disabled students isolate students from the mainstream at great cost and little benefit.

If you could give a piece of advice to someone who is about to enter this field, what would it be?

Make sure of the commitment that you need to make to enter this field.

See students' problems as part of a large perspective. Family dynamics play a large part in the ability to function as a student. Dysfunctional families perpetuate patterns of behavior that are not shed when family members leave for school or work in the morning.

Look for broad solutions to problems that seem to be narrow or limited in scope. Failing one English class may have large implications: what are staff perceptions towards disabled students, how appropriate is the curriculum, is reteaching or relooping part of the learning process, what innovations or resources need to be used to help students do better.

Supervisors in special education programs tend to find themselves torn between attending to student needs, hiring and supervising staff, and working with parents, teachers, and counselors. In general, supervisors are responsible for placing students in special education programs and developing individualized education programs to meet their needs. In order to serve their students effectively, supervisors must keep up with current developments and trends in all facets of special education: diagnosis, behavior modification, motivation, instruction, and assessment.

Another important part of a supervisor's job is to provide instructional leadership for the staff. A supervisor might demonstrate leadership by offering workshops on educational issues for staff or by working with staff members to solve specific classroom problems. Supervisors must provide staff members with accurate feedback on their performance, so they need to observe teachers in the classroom at least once a year and prepare formal evaluations. Supervisors must help teachers who need to improve their performance by developing plans to remediate problems.

When there are openings on the staff, supervisors must spend a great deal of time and energy sorting through applications, contacting possible candidates, conducting interviews, and helping to select the most promising candidates for the job. Supervisors also are responsible for planning and executing budgets and preparing reports for state and local school officials.

Most people who become special education supervisors enter the field as teachers. Typically, supervisors in special education spend years learning the process of teaching, behavior modification, and management skills, and they want to be in a position to help other teachers. Supervisors tend to have a more flexible schedule than classroom teachers, and they enjoy a wide variety of activities as part of their job. Many special education supervisors have a strong sense of how they want their programs to operate. They have a vision of what an effective school should look like, and they derive great satisfaction from the opportunity to make that vision come true. In almost all cases, supervisors are paid significantly more than the staff members that they supervise, although salary schedules can vary greatly from one community to another. Individual salaries will depend on the level of education and experience each supervisor has and on the number of employees that the supervisor has responsibility for.

The primary disadvantage of working as a supervisor in special education is the conflicting nature of the demands on the supervisor's time and energy. The whole process of special education tends to be extremely time consuming. Staffing young people into special education programs requires lengthy meetings with existing staff, students, and parents. Observing staff members to evaluate them properly requires an extensive time commitment.

Resolving staff problems and dealing with staff concerns is extremely time consuming. Maintaining a role as an instructional leader requires time for study and for continued professional growth. Supervisors also must deal with the emotional drains of working as a colleague, leader, and evaluator of staff. No matter how cordial a relationship may be, supervisors must be able to evaluate staff members accurately and objectively.

People who are interested in supervision must have strong communication and organizational skills. They must be able to focus on several issues at once and to prioritize their goals. Supervisors must be able to identify problems and work on ways to solve them. They also must develop clear goals as well as the ability to set limits and enforce them. Since supervision requires skills that are normally taught on the job, nearly all supervisors in special education begin their careers as teachers, attending classes for advanced degrees and administrative certificates during the summer or in the evenings. As with all professionals in special education, a bachelor's degree in education is the absolute minimum for work in this field. Supervisors commonly earn a master's degree in curriculum and supervision or a certificate of advanced study in supervision, and they are licensed by the state or province in which they work. This postgraduate work could amount to ten to twenty classes beyond the bachelor's degree.

Because special education teachers are professionals, very few supervisors are hired, and the competition for these jobs is usually keen. Successful candidates will have the appropriate credentials, and they will have demonstrated their leadership ability through committee work in the school, by working on projects that are aimed at improving instruction, or by participating in workshops or other professional growth activities.

CHAPTER 6

THE CLINICAL OR STUDENT TEACHING EXPERIENCE

"I guess I was too busy. All I wanted to do was pass my classes, get good grades, and get my work done on time. I never even thought about a job. The second semester of my senior year I got my credentials together for the placement office and just sort of waited for something to happen. It never did."

Earning a college diploma is hard work, and it's easy to become so focused on short-term goals like term papers and exams that you lose sight of your long-term goal: finding meaningful employment. From the moment that you decide that you want a career in special education until the time that you are working in your field, you must remain focused on your long-term goal: getting a job.

For professionals in special education, one important step in the process of getting a job is to make use of field training, clinical experiences, or student teaching. Everyone who aspires to work in special education will have to spend anywhere from nine to eighteen weeks working in a hospital, clinic, or school under the direct supervision of a professional. Many students feel imposed upon by this requirement because they have to pay tuition to the college during the student teaching period. Student teachers work forty hours a week, and they are not paid for their work. Although this can be very frustrating, please remember that if you approach your clinical experience in the right way, it can become a nine- to eighteen-week audition for a job. An innovative, energetic, responsible young professional can make a tremendous impression on colleagues and supervisors. The young people who complete teacher training or clinical experience at a school, hospital, or special education cooperative also have a sense of what the institution's goals and priorities are, and they have a sense of how the institution works. This insight makes them excellent candidates for a job. Personnel directors are comfortable hiring people who have completed clinical experiences in their institution because they can base their evaluation on an extended period of activity instead of relying on recommendations and a brief interview.

PLANNING FOR YOUR FUTURE

The student teaching/clinical experience can be very useful, but in order to make the best possible use of this experience, you need to plan in advance, and you need to think about some very important questions:

What do I want to do?

This is one question that we ask ourselves all the time. Special education is a very broad field, and as you think about your own interests and values, you need to make some decisions about what area of special education you want to specialize in. Think about the various job descriptions in the first section of this book, and take an inventory of your strengths.

- Do you have the patience that you need to work with students who cannot remember steps in a multistep problem?
- Do you have the patience to work with students who need repetition?

- Do you have the organizational skills to create a very structured environment for students who desperately need the structure?
- Can you develop individualized education plans for students who have vastly different needs?
- Do you have the emotional stamina to work with young people who are faced with terrible disabilities?
- Do you have the emotional stamina to work with people who might make progress in very small increments and who may regress?
- Do you have the physical stamina to work with people who may need physical or occupational therapy?
- What are your long-term goals? Where do you want to be in five or ten years? What do you want to be doing in five or ten years?

Once you have taken stock of your strengths and interests and determined the area of special education that appeals to you, you must consider a second, important question:

Where do I want to live?

Licensing and certification requirements vary from state to state in the United States, and almost as important, the school that you attend will have specific geographic boundaries for students who want to do clinical experiences. Colleges and universities simply cannot afford to send supervising professors all over the country to oversee their students. If you are determined to live in a specific part of the country after you graduate from college, plan to attend college and perform your clinical experience there. Appendixes A, B, and C of this book list colleges and universities that offer degrees in special education throughout the United States and Canada. Use this resource to help select a school in the part of the country where you want to spend your life. As you select your college or university, be sure to find out if you will have the opportunity to select the school, hospital, or special education cooperative at which you perform your clinical experience. If you have the opportunity to select the institution yourself, you are in a position to further your own career by selecting an institution that anticipates adding new staff in the immediate future.

Are they hiring?

Since your long-term goal is to find employment, and you want to use your clinical experience or student teaching as an audition for a job, you will want to perform that clinical experience at a school or hospital where there may be some job openings in the immediate future. In order to find out what institutions are expecting to add staff, you need to do a little research. This project might sound a little overwhelming, but if you allow yourself a generous time line and break the task into three manageable parts, it need not be terribly time consuming.

1. Gather information
2. Make an initial contact with the institution.
3. Write an introductory letter.

As you begin your junior year of college, start to gather information about schools or other facilities that you might use for your clinical experience. The institutions should be in the geographical area that appeals to you and within the boundaries that your college has set for sending supervising professors out for observation. There are several directories that will help you.

Addictions Recovery Resources List
American Network of Community Options
Billians Hospital Blue Book
BOSC Directory: Facilities for People with Learning Disabilities
Directory of Canadian Universities
Directory of Public Elementary and Secondary Education
    Agencies
Directory of Public School Systems in the United States

LAYING THE GROUNDWORK

Once you are armed with the addresses and phone numbers of these institutions, you need to sort through them and make a list of the places that you might be interested in using for your clinical experience. Get the list down to a manageable size, and make your initial contact. Before you can write anyone and ask about opportunities for student teaching, clinical experience, or future employment, you need to find out who you will be writing to. The process of calling personnel offices and asking who the personnel director is will take some time and cost some money, but it is an important step. Competent, professional people always know who they are writing or talking to.

You can save some time and money if you plan out what you want to say before you dial. Ask for the personnel office. Explain that you are a student in the field of special education, and that you want to write the agency and ask for some information about it. Therefore, you need to know how to spell the personnel director's name. Double-check the spelling, the title, and the mailing address and the zip code.

Your next step is to draft an informal but professional looking letter that asks for some information about the school district or agency. Explain that you are a student in the area of special education, and that as you are beginning to plan for your clinical experience, you want to be sure that you are as well prepared as possible. Ask about the kinds of skills and qualifications that the personnel director thinks a successful professional should have. Take a sentence or two to describe why you want to work in special education and discuss the kinds of experiences and training that you have. Be sure to ask the director's thoughts about a future in special education and if the director anticipates any openings in the near future. An informal letter might look something like this:

Dr. Anne Gordon
Northwest Special Education Cooperative
1411 North Morningside Street
Elk Grove Village, Illinois 60008

Dear Dr. Gordon:

Like many students in LD/BD, I am a little afraid that my course work is not enough preparation for my student teaching experience. If it is not too much of an imposition, I would like to call you and ask you some questions about the kinds of skills and qualifications you think a successful LD/BD teacher should have. I am beginning my junior year at Northern Illinois University, in DeKalb, and although I have enjoyed my course work and I have had the opportunity to volunteer as a reading aide at The Collins Center, I want to look for opportunities that will give me the skills that I need to do an excellent job. I would be grateful for any insights that you have on preparation, extracurricular activities, and opportunities for employment.

I know how busy you are, so I hope it will not be too great an imposition if I call your secretary and find a time when I could talk to you about these issues.

Sincerely,

Elizabeth Corcoran
403 South Market Street
DeKalb, Illinois 60160
(815) 555-0860

The content of the letter may be informal, but the format must be immaculate. Proofread carefully, and make revisions as needed. This is the first impression that the personnel director will have of you.

Misspellings, typos, errors in grammar or syntax can really work against you. Keep track of your responses, and when it is time to select a school or agency for your clinical experience, be sure to select one that will offer you the best opportunities for education and employment.

Many people have strong negative feelings about student teaching or clinical experiences. Some people have concerns about the costs of paying tuition and living expenses while working at an unpaid job. Other people are simply frightened of facing students in a real world situation. Try to get past these negative feelings. A clinical experience can offer you a wide range of learning opportunities. The way you make use of this experience can help you find the job you want. If you are student teaching, be sure to ask the best teachers in your area if you can borrow and use lessons, unit plans, teaching strategies and activities that they have developed. You may be able to adapt them for use later in your teaching career. Be sure to talk about situations and professional issues that concern you. Ask other professionals how they would deal with these concerns. The nine to eighteen weeks that you spend as part of your clinical experience can give you invaluable insights into your profession. If your clinical experience offers the opportunity for committee work or coaching, be sure to take advantage of it. All of these activities give you the opportunity to network with other professionals, establish a track record, and generate letters of recommendation from people who have actually seen you work. As you begin the process of applying for jobs, those recommendations will be extremely valuable to you.

GAINING EXPERIENCE

One question dominates the whole process of finding a position in special education:

Why should we hire you instead of somebody else?

Sometimes the question is asked out loud, sometimes it lingers in the air, sometimes it's only hinted at, but every successful applicant must be able to answer that question whether it's asked or not. And there is usually only one correct answer: "You should hire me because I have a proven track record of achievement in this field."

The successful applicant must be able to cite some specific accomplishments to back up that claim. But the difficulty new graduates in this field suffer from is the opportunity to gain experience in special education. Recent graduates often recite the old bromide about needing experience to get a job and needing a job to get experience. One way to approach this problem is to make careful use of summer and volunteer work.

Summer work in special education might involve work in day-care programs or summer activity programs. These programs offer an excellent opportunity to work in the field and to understand the special problems associated with this area. Summer work can provide an opportunity to develop the kinds of interpersonal skills that you will need in your career. The best opportunities will allow you to have contact with special education clients and with working professionals. Be sure to use this time to observe the ways in which these professionals work with their clients. Make note of ideas, strategies, and techniques that seem to be very effective.

If your work setting is fairly informal, you may be able to use your summer work as an opportunity to network with other professionals in your area. Every workplace has its own, often unwritten rules about communication between permanent and temporary staff, but if you can find a professional who is willing to talk about serious issues in this field, you can network and learn a great deal at the same time.

At the end of your summer job, be sure to ask someone you respect to write you a letter of recommendation. Every letter of recommendation that you acquire helps to document your growth as a professional.

Volunteer work is another way to gain valuable experience. Many students are reluctant to consider volunteer work because they feel pressed by course loads or the need to hold down a part-time job. Carefully selected volunteer work can yield many benefits. Certainly the most tangible benefit is that anyone who reads your resume will know that you are going into the field of special education because you genuinely care about people who have special needs. You want to make a positive impact on people who need you; you are not just looking for a paycheck and a long summer vacation.

Another important benefit of volunteer work is that you can choose the kind of experience that will help you the most. In your work with special needs clients and with professionals, you will get the benefit of observing practitioners at work. If you volunteer consistently you can develop a network of professionals who can recommend you based on their observation of your performance. If you decide to volunteer, think about the kind of experience that you need to grow as a professional. Once you decide on the kind of experience that will help you, take a look at your schedule. You will need a short block of time that you can donate on a regular basis for a semester or for a school year. Once you know what you want to do and how much time you can give, look at the special education schools, special education cooperatives, drug and alcohol rehabilitation facilities, and hospitals in your area to find one agency that can give you the kind of volunteer experience that you want and that is close enough to allow you to commute.

Personnel directors are sometimes hesitant to accept volunteers. Confidentiality and liability are important considerations, and there is always the concern that volunteers may fail to follow through after they have been oriented and trained by the paid staff. In these cases, volunteers actually can deplete an agency's resources. You can allay a lot of concerns by the way that you approach the agency. In general, you need to follow the same procedures that you used to select the school or facility for your student teaching or clinical experience. Select an agency. Find out the director or principal's name. Double-check the spelling and address. Write a short letter that explains why you are interested in special education, what you are willing to do, how much time you can give, and how long you can continue to volunteer. Use a sentence or two to explain why you need a volunteer experience to enhance your own education. The administrator needs to know that you are volunteering because you want to be there, not because you have been sentenced to community service. Your letter might look something like this:

Dr. Gwen Schumacher
Director, The Collins Center
2109 North First Street
DeKalb, Illinois 60160

Dear Dr. Schumacher:

As a sophomore special education major at Northern Illinois University, I am concerned that the theories that I am learning will not make much sense unless I have a chance to work with special education clients. I need to see the connection between the skills my professors talk about and the needs special education clients have. I would be very interested in volunteering at The Collins Center as an activity aide. My course schedule gives me a two-hour block of time on Tuesdays and Thursdays from 1:00 until 3:00 P.M. My schedule may change in January, but I can be available every Tuesday and Thursday from now until then.

I know that many schools and agencies are hesitant to use volunteers because they sometimes fail to follow through on their commitments. I understand their reluctance, but I can tell you that I have been interested in special education since I was in high school, and I view the opportunity to work with your clients and staff as an important learning experience. If you accept me as a volunteer at The Collins Center, I will live up to my commitment.

Sincerely,

Elizabeth Corcoran
403 South Market Street
DeKalb, Illinois 60160

Once you begin your volunteer work, be careful to be punctual and to show up when you are scheduled. Use this opportunity to work with professionals. If your situation permits, use this time to talk with working professionals about issues in your field. This is an excellent way to begin a network of professional people whom you can turn to for advice or who can provide valuable information about career opportunities. Before your volunteer experience ends, ask for a letter of recommendation from the agency director or from someone that you have worked with and respect. A recommendation from a working professional carries a great deal of weight and will help establish you as a competent, serious professional.

CHAPTER 7

THE APPLICATION PROCESS

RESUMES

"Why should I hire you instead of somebody else?"

"Because I have a record of success in this field."

Now that you have invested the time and energy needed to build a resume, you need to present your qualifications effectively. Unfortunately, many people are so intimidated by the thought of "bragging" about themselves that they fail to provide potential employers with the information that might get them a job. Others are so worried about the format of the resume and the need to compress education and experience into a short, readable form that they delete important information just to make all the information fit on one page. Before you start to work on your resume, take the time to answer a few questions:

1. What kind of job are you looking for?
2. Where do you want to work?
3. What work or volunteer experience do you have?
4. How does that experience relate to what you want to do?
5. What academic credentials do you have?
6. Is your school noted for its research or programs in special education?

7. Does your school have the kind of prestige that makes a personnel director want to read your resume?
8. Have you achieved any special recognition for your studies or volunteer work?
9. Why do you want this particular job? What is it about this organization's philosophy, location, or salary that makes it special?

Once you have answered these questions, think about your strengths as a potential employee. As you develop your resume, you must emphasize these strengths. Many people are intimidated by the process of developing a resume, but the mechanics of a resume are fairly straightforward. There are five basic elements of a resume: heading, experience, education, awards, and, finally, references.

Heading

This information includes your name, an address where you can always be reached, and a phone number for an answering machine or answering service.

Experience

You need to make one of your first important decisions here. If your strengths lie in experience, lead with it. If your strengths lie in your academic preparation, list that information first.

When you discuss your work experience, be careful to discuss jobs that directly relate to the job that you want. Although resumes need to be brief, you shortchange yourself if you do not spend a sentence or two discussing the job responsibilities that relate to the job you want. The personnel director who reads your resume needs to see a connection between the volunteer or work experience at which you have been successful in the past and the kinds of responsibilities that a new job might entail. A simple list of places where you worked and dates of employment may not be of much help. If you are applying for a position in a school, make sure that you include any coaching or extracurricular experience that you have acquired.

Education

All of the jobs that we have discussed so far require academic credentials, and many of these jobs also require a state license. Although it may not seem very logical, personnel directors receive resumes from people who apply for jobs but don't have the academic credentials to be hired for them. A personnel director must be able to scan your resume and find out what you are licensed to do. Be sure to include the name and address of the college or university that you attended and the dates you earned your degrees. List your licenses separately and be sure that you include the date that you earned them.

In addition to your license and degrees, be sure to discuss any teachable minor areas of study. If you participated in any special activities in college—as a teaching assistant, peer tutor, or member of any college team—you need to include that information as well. The athletic, academic, and leadership skills that you developed in these activities can be very useful in any profession.

Honors and Awards

If you received a scholarship, or if you have been recognized for leadership or service, be sure to record that information on your resume. Even though the awards may not directly relate to your career goal, anything that demonstrates a willingness to assume responsibility or provide leadership helps prospective employers see you as an asset to their organization.

Work on the rough draft of your resume. Don't be afraid to use more than one page. You need to provide specific information about your experience and show credentials that will encourage a personnel director to call you in for an interview. Don't delete inportant information just to keep your resume short.

There are several possible resume formats to choose from. Spend an hour or so looking at different formats and rearranging the information on them until you find a format that works for you. Please remember that the format is less important than careful attention to spelling, grammar, punctuation, and factual detail. It is important that you resist the temptation to embroider your resume with half truths or outright lies. Don't claim awards of experience that you don't have. Many personnel directors have excellent skills when it comes to reading body language. It is very likely that they will sense that something is wrong when they ask about credentials that you don't really have. Even if you are able to fabricate your way into a job, the stress of worrying about being exposed is not worth any advantage that a fraudulent resume can buy you.

References

If you have taken the time to ask for a recommendation from every one of the employers that you listed on your resume, copy the letters and attach them to your resume. If you have any letters pertaining to your volunteer experience, student teaching, clinical experience, or cocurricular activities, copy and attach those letters as well. You also will have a file of recommendations from professors and supervisors at your clinical experience. These letters will probably be confidential, so you must offer to have your placement file sent to the personnel director on request. The following sample resume might be a good starting point for your own efforts.

Elizabeth Anne Corcoran
828 North Dunton Street
Arlington Heights, Illinois 60004
(708) 555-2036

Objective	To work with learning disabled and behavior disordered students.
Experience	1992–1994: The Collins Center, 2901 North First Street, DeKalb, Illinois. I volunteered as an activity aide at The Collins Center for two years. I worked with LD/BD students as an aide and as a tutor two afternoons a week.
	1993 and 1994: Michaels Y.M.C.A., 1529 Rand Road, Palatine, Illinois. I worked as an activity aide for the summer program for handicapped youth from June until September.
	1990–1994: Peer Tutor, Northern Illinois University, DeKalb, Illinois. I tutored students in reading and social sciences one afternoon a week for the four years that I was enrolled at Northern.
Education	1990–1994: Northern Illinois University, DeKalb, Illinois. B.S. in education, 1994.
Certification	I am certified to teach learning disabled and behavior disordered students.
Honors and Awards	Outstanding Senior Award, College of Education, Northern Illinois University, 1994.
	Outstanding Volunteer 1994, The Collins Center, DeKalb, Illinois.
References	Dr. Gwen Schumacher, Director, The Collins Center, 2109 North First Street, DeKalb, Illinois 60160.

Dr. Phillip Armbruster, Professor of Education, Northern Illinois University, DeKalb, Illinois 60160.

Dr. James Jackson, Director, Behavior Education Center, 2201 South Goebbert Road, Arlington Heights, Illinois 60004.

Mr. Mark Thompson, Director, Michaels Y.M.C.A., 1529 Rand Road, Palatine, Illinois 60067.

COVER LETTERS

In order to make the maximum impact, your resume must be accompanied by a cover letter that is addressed to the personnel director of the agency that you are applying to. The cover letter should explain why you want to work for that particular organization. The cover letter will be similar to the letter that you developed when you were surveying agencies for your clinical experience. Be sure to include any professional growth, such as conferences or programs that you have attended, and be sure to discuss any pertinent work experience that you think makes you a good candidate for the job. Make sure that you have proofread this letter carefully. This is not a time for poor spelling or sloppy grammar.

The obvious disadvantage of writing a personalized letter to each personnel director is that it take time, and job applicants often equate a careful job search with the total number of resumes sent out. Please remember that personnel directors are not looking for someone who needs a job; they are looking for someone who will fit their organization's particular needs and someone who wants to work for their particular organization. Careful research and personalized letters may be far more useful that any scattershot approach.

An appropriate cover letter might look something like this:

Dr. Angela Martin
Assistant Superintendent for Personnel
High School District 511
North Brookfield, Illinois 62210

Dear Dr. Martin:

I was delighted when Dr. James Jackson of the Behavior Education Center suggested that there might be a job opening this fall for an LD/BD teacher at the B.E.C. My student teaching experience at the B.E.C. was such a challenging and satisfying experience that I would love to continue my relationship with the center as a teacher. Over the last several years, I have had the opportunity to observe teachers and students at many schools, but the sense of optimism, the level of caring, and the professionalism of the staff at B.E.C. makes me want to be part of that team. I am enclosing my resume, and I hope that after you review my volunteer and work experience, I will have the opportunity to meet with you in an interview.

Sincerely,

Elizabeth Corcoran
828 North Dunton Street
Arlington Heights, Illinois 60004
(708) 555-2036

THE PLACEMENT OFFICE

The first contact most students have with their college placement office or career center usually comes in the second semester of their senior year, when they are in the process of putting their placement files together. A college placement office will maintain a confidential file of student transcripts and recommendations, but that is only one of the many services that may be available. Placements offices may offer vocational interest inventories, career counseling, and aptitude tests. In most colleges, the placement office is a clearinghouse for job information. Many schools produce newsletters with job listings as they come in. In order to derive the most benefit from your college placement office, be sure to start visiting it early in your senior year. Find out what services are available, and get your credentials in order. If your school producers a mailing list of job listings, make sure that you subscribe to it.

APPLICATIONS

Typically a school district or other organization will send out job applications after receiving your resume and cover letter. Wading through a job application can be a very frustrating and time-consuming process, especially since the application always asks for the exact same information that you spent hours organizing in your resume. Be patient. School districts, hospitals, special education cooperatives, and other agencies that employ licensed professionals are require to keep meticulous records. By using a standard employment application, they can keep track of hundreds of pieces of information and retrieve them when accrediting agencies want to inspect their records. As you type or print the information on your application, be sure that all of the information is accurate. Personnel directors will verify education and employment information, so be sure to include names, addresses, zip codes, and phone numbers.

Essays

Because of the problems with grade inflation and trophy transcripts, some employers require a short essay as part of their application. Two obvious questions to expect will be why you want to work in special education, and why you want to work for this particular organization. Because of the demanding nature of special education, personnel directors are looking for a good job match, a linkup between a person who needs to help people, and a job that requires a long-term emotional and intellectual commitment. An essay can provide that information. Essays also tell personnel directors a great deal about an applicant's communication skills and organizational ability. The essay is not just intended as busy work or as just another hoop to jump through, so take your time and draft a thoughtful, honest response to the questions you are asked.

You have already done a great deal of the groundwork for your essay. Look at a copy of your resume and at the copies of the letters that you wrote requesting placement as a volunteer. Reread the letter you wrote before you selected the right organization for your clinical experience. You will be able to pull a great deal of material from these sources. As you write your essay, be sure to consider two very important points:

1. The ideal essay tells a personnel director that you want to work in that one particular organization. In order to do that, you will need some specific information about that school district, hospital, or agency. Is there a special program or innovative strategy that the agency is noted for? Have any of the administrators published anything in academic or medical journals? Has anyone in the agency given a speech, presented a program at a conference, or developed a program that other professionals are aware of? This is a good time to use your network of family, friends, professors, supervising teachers, and former or current job supervisors to get information about the agency you are applying to. If you have taken the time to research the organization, there is a good chance that people in the organization will want to interview you.

2. Remember that part of your essay must discuss your reasons for entering the field of special education. You need to think about why you are attracted to this demanding career, and you must be able to describe how your volunteer and paid work experience in special education has helped to prepare you for employment in the field. You may feel uncomfortable describing your credentials, because we all have ingrained reservations about bragging. As you describe your qualifications, remember, you are not bragging. You are helping professionals make an important decision. A sample essay might look something like this:

> I started working with handicapped children when I was in high school. I tutored fifth grade students at Olive School as part of my self project. I remember how frustrated the children were and how much they wanted to catch up with their friends in class. I wished that I had the skills to help them meet their goals.
>
> I earned my B.S. Ed. at Northern Illinois University in DeKalb, Illinois. I have a dual certificate in LD and BD. I wanted to add a practical dimension to my studies, so I volunteered to tutor students at Northern as part of the peer tutoring program, and I volunteered to work as an activity aide at The Collins Center. I volunteered for two afternoons a week for the past two years. I enjoyed working with the students and staff at The Collins Center. It was a wonderful opportunity to watch professionals use the theories that my professors discussed in class. The time I spent as an activity aide helped me learn how to work with disabled students, and the staff taught me some valuable teaching strategies and motivational techniques.
>
> Undoubtedly, the best part of my teacher training was the eighteen weeks that I spent as a student teacher at the Behavior Education Center. I was touched by the sense of optimism at the center. Dr. Jackson's commitment to mainstreaming students as soon as possible, and the staff's willingness to experiment with new approaches and moti-

vators in order to help students finally be able to "catch up" with their peers in regular education makes the B.E.C. a leader in special education. I would like to spend my professional life working with the students and staff at the Behavior Education Center.

EXPANDING THE JOB SEARCH

While you are in the process of following up on job leads that are generated by your college's placement office or that you hear about through your network, be sure to expand your job search by contacting lesser-known agencies that might be able to offer you full- or part-time work. Some agencies that you might wish to explore are:

Public Schools: There are several directories that will help you locate public and private schools.

Directory of Public Elementary and Secondary Education Agencies in the United States
Directory of Canadian Universities
Directory of Public School Systems in the United States
Education and Hiring Guide for Alaska, Hawaii, Idaho, Nevada, Montana, Oregon, Utah, Washington, and Wyoming
Pattersons American Education
Private Independent Schools
Private Independent Schools in the United States
The Canadian Almanack

Hospitals: Many hospitals need professionals with a background in special education to work with school-age patients. Working conditions and salaries will vary from hospital to hospital, but in many cases hospitals offer very competitive hourly wages.

Billians Hospital Blue Book

Residential Treatment Programs: Residential programs that work with school-age children need teachers and other special education professionals to meet the needs of their clients. Working conditions and salaries may vary dramatically, but these programs offer an opportunity to help young people and to develop professional skills.

Addiction and Recovery Resources

County Jails and State and Federal Prisons: Many penal institutions will offer education and therapy as part of their program. Although working in a jail or prison can be a very demanding job, it is an opportunity to help people who really need help.

Directory of Juvenile and Adult Correctional Departments, Institutions, Agencies and Paroling Authorities

CHAPTER 8

THE INTERVIEW

PREPARING FOR THE INTERVIEW

You send out resumes and cover letters, you send out applications and credentials files, you sift through letters of rejection, and you wait by the phone for someone, anyone, to call. Then suddenly the phone rings, and a polite person on the other end of the line asks when it would be convenient for you to stop by for an interview. After fifteen minutes of delirious joy, your stomach begins to knot up. You are now face to face with the dreaded interview. For a few moments your mind races through every nightmarish mistake you can possible make during an interview. If possible, you are more anxious than before the phone rang.

Everyone is frightened by the prospect of a face-to-face interview, partly because we know that we have a lot at stake. Since the interview process is so time consuming, personnel directors spend a great deal of time sorting through the applications to prepare a short list of applicants to interview. The personal interview is probably the most crucial step in obtaining the job we want. So even though it is normal to be anxious about the interview, it is important to invest that energy in preparing for it, instead of torturing ourselves about it.

No matter what form the interview will take, the interviewer will be looking for some specific information about your skills, experience, and attitudes. The best way to prepare for an interview is to anticipate the kinds of questions the interviewer will ask. Expect questions on:

Academic Preparation: What are you licensed to do? What clients are you licensed to serve?

Experience: How has your volunteer experience, work experience, or supervised clinical experience prepared you to do the job that you are applying for? Think of specific examples of problems that you faced and solutions that you tried. Be prepared to talk about your successes and about the kinds of lessons that you learned from your failures. Think about specific skills and techniques that you learned in your training and experience, and be prepared to discuss them.

Attitudes: The interviewer will be very concerned about your attitudes towards work and towards other people. Most jobs in special education require tremendous self discipline. There is very little day-to-day supervision in this field. Supervisors have to trust their employees to live up to their professional obligations. The interviewer is looking for someone who is strongly self-directed, who is willing to invest personal time on professional growth, and who will ask for help when necessary but who, in general, works independently. As you prepare for your interview, think of examples that can demonstrate this kind of self-motivated behavior.

The interviewer also will be very interested in your concern for other people and in your ability to work with young people and adults. Special education is essentially a service industry. People in this field must be able to empathize, set limits, encourage change, and reward appropriate behavior. This career requires tolerance, compassion, and concern for young people. As you prepare for your interview, be sure to think about specific examples of this behavior.

No one may actually ask the question, but the real question that you must answer is, "Why should we hire you instead of somebody else?" Think about that question, and be able to explain why your skills, experience, and attitudes make you the best possible choice for this job.

It's normal to be anxious about the interview, but remember that the people who will interview you will be much more uncomfortable than you are. For you the interview represents a few hours of investment in time and stress. However, the people who hire you are making a long-term commitment. In many cases they will have to live with their choice for the rest of their professional lives. Behavior that might appear to be cold or condescending may actually just be fear. Most personnel directors are confident professionals who have developed an arsenal of questions that will give them the information that they need, but it is possible that a personnel director may be distracted by ill health or personal issues. Or, perhaps the committee charged with conducting the interview is so overwhelmed by the process of selecting staff that they fail to ask the right questions, the questions that allow you to talk about your particular strengths. In order to deal with this situation, you need to make a short list of the points that you would like to make during your interview. If the interviewer fails to ask the right questions, be sure to bring the points up yourself. Include these points as part of the answers to other questions or near the close of the interview, when the interviewer asks if you have any questions or comments.

CONDUCTING THE INTERVIEW

After you have prepared for your interview, be sure to attend to a few important details.

Know Where You Are Going: You don't need the stress of consulting maps and asking for directions as the time for your interview draws nearer and nearer. If you are not absolutely certain of the location, make a point in advance to drive past the place where the interview will take place.

Be on Time: Plan to allow yourself fifteen minutes to go to the bathroom, freshen up, and relax before you start your interview.

Dress Professionally: Although many employees at schools and social service agencies dress casually, remember that they can afford to—they already have the job. Dress for the interview like a young professional in the business world. As a general rule of thumb, don't wear anything that will distract you from answering questions, such as shoes or ties that are too tight. Don't wear anything that will distract the interviewer from your answers.

Calm Down: Be calm, confident, and relaxed. You have taken the time to prepare for this interview. You have the list of the points that you want to make during the interview, and you are speaking to people who genuinely want you to be successful. You have done everything you can to ensure your success. Relax and enjoy the opportunity to talk to professionals in your field. No matter how the interview goes, you will have a valuable learning experience behind you.

Listen: Take time to listen to the questions. Don't cut people off before they are finished speaking. Don't answer until you have a chance to think about what you are being asked. This is not a quiz show with the prize going to whomever hits the buzzer first. Take the time to listen carefully, understand what the interviewer wants, and phrase your answer. The interviewer has taken some time to think about what to ask, and it is perfectly reasonable to take your time with a carefully considered answer.

Follow Up: When the interview is over, be sure to telephone or write a short note thanking the personnel director for the opportunity to come in for an interview. The few minutes it takes to follow up on an interview are well invested. The follow-up note or phone call can be a second chance for you. The note you write or call you make can be the means by which you mention any points that you overlooked during your interview. The small amount of extra effort required for a follow-up call or note also lets the personnel director know that you are genuinely interested in the job, that you are not just looking at the interview as a practice session.

AVOIDING THE EMOTIONAL ROLLER COASTER

Living through a job search is one of the most emotionally draining, frustrating events in anyone's life. It is very easy to look at every rejection letter and every interview as a referendum on your worth as a human being. Please remember that the interviewer or the interview committee is looking for a good job match. No one looks at an interview as an oral exam, with the job as a prize for the contestant who gets the most right answers. The goal is to find an applicant who has the skills that are needed, who can work with the existing staff, and who can bring a particular set of values and attitudes to the organization. Interviews are frustrating because the people who advertise the jobs and conduct the interviews may not be able to describe the exact qualities that they are looking for. It's impossible to do an accurate postmortem after the interview and determine just how well you have done, because you don't have all the information that you need. All you can do is prepare, answer the questions honestly, and then concentrate on the next application or interview.

UNIVERSITIES THAT OFFER DEGREES IN SPECIAL EDUCATION

Following is an alphabetical list of universities in the United States and Canada that offer degrees in special education:

Alabama

Alabama A and M University
P.O. Box 284
Normal, 35762

Alabama State University
P.O. Box 271-915
South Jackson Street
Montgomery, 36101-0271

Athens State College
P.O. Box 2216
Beaty Street
Athens, 36849

Auburn University
Mary E. Martin Hall
Auburn, 36849

Jacksonville State University
700 Pelham Road North
Jacksonville, 36265-9982

Tallemeda College
637 West Battle Street
Talladega, 35160

Troy State University
University Avenue
Troy, 36082

Tuskegee University
Carnagie Hall
Tuskegee, 36088

University of Alabama
Box 870132
Tuscaloosa, 35487-0132

University of Alabama-
    Birmingham
  University Station
  Birmingham, 35294

University of Northern
    Alabama
  Wesleyan Avenue
  Florence, 35632

University of Southern
    Alabama
  307 University Boulevard
  Mobile, 36688

Alberta

University of Alberta
  Edmonton, Alberta
  Canada T6G 2E8

University of Calgary
  2500 University Drive NW
  Calgary, Alberta
  Canada T2N 1N4

University of Lethbridge
  4401 University Drive
  Lethbridge, Alberta
  Canada T1K 3M4

Arizona

Arizona State University
  Tempe, 85287-0112

Grand Canyon University
  3300 West Camelback Road
  Phoenix, 85017

Northern Arizona University
  Box 4084
  Flagstaff, 86011

Arkansas

Arkansas State University
  P.O. Box 1630
  State University, 72467

Harding University
  Box 762-Station A
  Searcy, 72143

Henderson State University
  Arkadelphia, 71923

John Brown University
  Siloam Springs, 72761

Philander Smith College
  812 West Thirteenth Street
  Little Rock, 72202

Southern Arkansas University
  Administration 222
  Fayetteville, 72701

University of Arkansas-
    Monticello
  Monticello, 71655

University of Arkansas-
  Pine Bluff
  1200 University Drive
  Pine Bluff, 71601-2799

University of Central
  Arkansas
  Conway, 72032

British Columbia

University of British
  Columbia
  Vancouver, British
  Columbia
  Canada V6T 1Z2

University of Victoria
  P.O. Box 1700
  Victoria, British Columbia
  Canada U8W 2Y2

California

California State University-
  Dominguez Hills
  Carson, 90747

California State University-
  Fresno
  Shaw and Cedar Avenues
  Fresno, 93740

California State University-
  Sacramento
  6000 J Street
  Sacramento, 95819

California State University-
  Stanislaus
  801 West Monte Vista
  Avenue
  Turlock, 95380

Humboldt State University
  Arcata, 95819

LaSierra University
  4700 Pierce Street
  Riverside, 92515

San Diego State University
  5300 Campanile Drive
  San Diego, 92182

San Francisco State
  University
  1600 Holloway Avenue
  San Francisco, 94132

Southern California College
  55 Fair Drive
  Costa Mesa, 92626

University of California-
  Irvine
  Irvine, 92717

University of California-
  Riverside
  1100 Administration
  Building
  Riverside, 92521

University of LaVerne
  1950 Third Street
  LaVerne, 91750

University of the Pacific
  3601 Pacific Avenue
  Stockton, 90608

Whittier College
  13406 East Philadelphia
  Whittier, 90608

Colorado

Adams State College
  Alamosa, 81102

University of Colorado-
  Boulder
  Campus Box B-7
  Boulder, 80309

University of Colorado-
  Denver
  Campus Box 167-
  1200 Larimer
  Denver, 80204

University of Northern
  Colorado
  Greeley, 80639

Connecticut

Central Connecticut State
  University
  1615 Stanely Street
  New Britain, 06050

Southern Connecticut State
  University
  501 Crescent Street
  New Haven, 06515

University of Connecticut
  Storrs, 06269

University of Hartford
  200 Bloomfield Avenue
  West Hartford, 06117

Delaware

Delaware State College
  1200 North DuPont
  Highway
  Dover, 19901

University of Delaware
  116 Hullihen Hall
  Newark, 19716

District of Columbia

Trinity College
  Michigan Avenue and
  Franklin Avenue NE
  Washington, DC 20017

University of the District of
  Columbia
  4200 Connecticut Avenue
  NW
  Washington, DC 20008

Florida

Bethune-Cookman College
640 Second Avenue
Daytona Beach, 32015

Edward Waters College
1659 Kings Road
Jacksonville, 32209

Flagler College
P.O. Box 1027
St. Augustine, 32085

Florida Atlantic University
P.O. Box 3091
Boca Raton, 33431-0991

Florida International
University
University Park
Miami, 33199

Florida Southern College
111 Lake Hollingsworth
Drive
Lakeland, 33801

Florida State University
Tallahassee, 32306

Jacksonville University
2800 University Boulevard
Jacksonville, 32211

Palm Beach Atlantic College
1101 South Olive Avenue
West Palm Beach, 33401

Saint Leo College
P.O. Box 20008
Saint Leo, 33574

University of Central Florida
P.O. Box 25000
Orlando, 32816

University of Miami
P.O. Box 248025
Coral Gables, 33124

University of North Florida
P.O. Box 17074
Jacksonville, 32216

University of South Florida
4202 Fowler Avenue
Tampa, 33620

University of West Florida
11000 University Parkway
Pensacola, 32514

Georgia

Albany State College
504 College Drive
Albany, 31705

Armstrong State College
11935 Abercorn Street
Savannah, 31419

Augusta College
2500 Walton Way
Augusta, 30910

Columbus College
    Algonquin Drive-
        Richards Building
    Columbus, 31993

Fort Valley State College
    805 State College Drive
    Fort Valley, 31030

Georgia Southern University
    Box 8024
    Statesboro, 30458

Georgia Southwestern
    Wheatley Street
    Americus, 31709

Georgia State University
    University Plaza
    Atlanta, 30303

Mercer University
    1400 Coleman Avenue
    Macon, 31207

Morris Brown College
    643 Martin Luther King Jr.
        Drive NW
    Atlanta, 30317

North Georgia College
    Dahlonega, 30597

Piedmont College
    Demorest, 30535

University of Georgia
    114 Academic Building
    Athens, 30602

Valdosta State College
    1500 North Patterson Street
    Valdosta, 31698

West Georgia College
    Carrolton, 30118

Idaho

Boise State University
    1910 University Drive
    Boise, 83725

Idaho State University
    P.O. Box 8054
    Pocatello, 83209

Lewis Clark State College
    Eighth Avenue and Sixth
        Street
    Lewiston, 83501

University of Idaho
    Moscow, 83843

Illinois

Barat College
    700 East Westleigh Road
    Lake Forest, 60045

Blackburn College
    700 College Avenue
    Carlinville, 62626

Bradley University
  1501 West Bradley
  Peoria, 61625

Chicago State University
  Ninety-fifth Street at King
    Drive
  Chicago, 60628

Eastern Illinois University
  Old Main-Room 116
  Charleston, 61920

Elmhurst College
  190 Prospect Avenue
  Elmhurst, 60126-3296

Greenville College
  315 East College Avenue
  Greenville, 62246

Illinois Benedictine College
  5700 College Road
  Lisle, 60532

Illinois State University
  201 Hovey Hall
  Normal, 61761

Lewis University
  Route 53
  Romeoville, 60441

Loyola University of Chicago
  820 North Michigan
    Avenue
  Chicago, 60611

MacMurry College
  447 East College Street
  Jacksonville, 62650

Monmouth College
  700 East Broadway
  Monmouth, 61462

National Lewis University
  2840 Sheridan Road
  Evanston, 60201

Northeastern Illinois
    University
  5500 North St. Louis
    Avenue
  Chicago, 60625

Northern Illinois University
  Dekalb, 60115

Northwestern University
  P.O. Box 3060-
    1801 Hinman Avenue
  Evanston, 60201-3060

Quincy University
  1800 College Avenue
  Quincy, 62301

Southern Illinois University
    at Carbondale
  Woody Hall
  Carbondale, 62901

Southern Illinois University
at Edwardsville
Box 1047
Edwardsville, 62026

St. Xavier University
3700 West 103rd Street
Chicago, 60655

University of Illinois at
Urbana-Champaign
506 South Wright Street
Urbana, 61801

Western Illinois University
900 West Adams Street
Macomb, 61455-1383

Indiana

Anderson University
Anderson, 46012

Ball State University
2000 University Avenue
Muncie, 47306

Butler University
Forty-sixth and Sunset
Avenue
Indianapolis, 46208

Franklin College
Monroe Street
Franklin, 46131

Indiana State University
217 North Sixth Street
Terre Haute, 47809

Indiana University-
Bloomington
314 East Third Street
Bloomington, 47405

Indiana University-Kokomo
P.O. Box 9003
Kokomo, 46904-9003

Indiana University-Northwest
3400 Broadway
Gary, 46408

Indiana University-
South Bend
P.O. Box 7111-
1700 Mishawaka Avenue
South Bend, 46634

Indiana University-Southeast
4201 Grant Line Road
New Albany, 47150

Marian College
3200 Cold Spring Road
Indianapolis, 46222

Purdue University
Schleman Hall
West Lafayette, 47907

Purdue University-Calumet
2233 171st Street
Hammond, 46323

St. Francis College
2701 Spring Street
Fort Wayne, 46808

St. Mary of the Woods
College
St. Mary of the Woods,
47876

University of Evansville
1800 East Lincoln Avenue
Evansville, 47722

University of Indianapolis
1400 East Hanna Avenue
Indianapolis, 46227

Valparaiso University
Valparaiso, 46383

Iowa

Buena Vista College
610 West Fourth Street
Storm Lake, 50588

Central College
812 University Street
Pella, 50219

Clarke College
1550 Clarke Drive
Dubuque, 52001

Iowa State University
Alumni Hall
Ames, 50011

Loras College
1450 Alta Vista
Dubuque, 52001

Morningside College
1501 Morningside Avenue
Sioux City, 51106

Northwestern College
101 College Avenue
Orange City, 51041

St. Ambrose College
518 West Locust Street
Davenport, 52803

University of Dubuque
2000 University Avenue
Dubuque, 52001

University of Northern Iowa
West Twenty-seventh Street
Cedar Falls, 50614

Wartburg College
P.O. Box 1003-
222 Ninth Street NW
Waverly, 50677

Kansas

Benedictine College
North Campus
Atchison, 66002

Bethel College
  300 East Twenty-seventh
    Street
  North Newton, 67117

Emporia State University
  Twelfth and Commercial
    Streets
  Emporia, 66801

Fort Hayes State University
  600 Park Street
  Hays, 67601

Kansas Wesleyan University
  100 East Clarifin
  Salina, 67401

McPherson College
  1600 East Euclid
  McPherson, 67460

Pittsburg State University
  1701 South Broadway
  Pittsburg, 66762

Saint Mary College
  4100 South Fourth Street
  Leavenworth, 66048

Sterling College
  North Broadway
  Sterling, 67579

Tabor College
  Hillsboro, 67073

Wichita State University
  8545 Fairmount Street
  Wichita, 67208

Kentucky

Bellarmine College
  2001 Newburg Road
  Louisville, 40205-0671

Brescia College
  717 Frederica Street
  Owensboro, 42301

Cumberland College
  6178 College Station Drive
  Williamsburg, 40769

Eastern Kentucky University
  Lancaster Avenue
  Richmond, 40475

Morehead State University
  Morehead, 40351

Murray State University
  Murray, 42071

Northern Kentucky University
  Nunn Drive
  Highland Heights,
    41099-7010

Pikeville College
  Sycamore Street
  Pikeville, 41501

University of Kentucky
  100 Funkhouser Building
  Lexington, 4050

University of Louisville
  Louisville, 40292

Western Kentucky University
  Wetherby Administration
    Building, Room 209
  Bowling Green, 42101

Louisiana

Dillard University
  2601 Gentilly Boulevard
  New Orleans, 70122-3097

Grambling State University
  Grambling, 71245

Louisiana College
  P.O. Box 560
  Pineville, 71359

Louisiana State University
  110 Thomas Boyd Hall
  Baton Rouge, 70803

Louisiana State University-
    Shreveport
  One University Place
  Shreveport, 71115

Louisiana Tech University
  P.O. Box 3168 Tech Station
  Ruston, 71272

NcNeese State University
  P.O. Box 92495
  Lake Charles, 70603

Nicholls State University
  P.O. Box 2004 University
    Station
  Thibodaux, 70310

Northeast Louisiana
    University
  700 University Avenue
  Monroe, 71209

Northwestern State
    University of Louisiana
  College Avenue
  Natchitoches, 71497

Southeastern Louisiana
    University
  Box 752-University Station
  Hammond, 70402

Southern University-
    Baton Rouge
  P.O. Box 9901-
    Southern Branch
  Baton Rouge, 70813

University of Southwestern
    Louisiana
  P.O. Box 41770
  Lafayette, 70504

Xavier University of
   Louisiana
7325 Palmetto Street
New Orleans, 70125

Maine

University of Maine at
   Farmington
102 Main Street
Farmington, 04938

Manitoba

University of Manitoba
   Winnipeg, Manitoba
   Canada R3T 2N2

Maryland

Bowie State University
   Jericho Park Road
   Bowie, 20715

College of Notre Dame of
   Maryland
4701 North Charles Street
Baltimore, 21210

Coppin State College
   2500 West North Avenue
   Baltimore, 21216

Goucher College
   1021 Dulaney Valley Road
   Baltimore, 21204

Hood College
   Rosemont Avenue
   Frederick, 21701

Loyola College
   4501 North Charles Street
   Baltimore, 21210

University of Maryland at
   College Park
   College Park, 20742

University of Maryland-
   Eastern Shore
   Princess Anne, 21853

Massachusetts

American International
   College
1000 State Street
Springfield, 01109

Boston College
   Lyons Hall-Room 120
   Chestnut Hill, 02167

Bridgewater State College
   Bridgewater, 02325

Curry College
   1071 Blue Hill Road
   Milton, 02186

Fitchburg State College
   160 Pearl Street
   Fitchburg, 01420

Gordon College
255 Grapevine Road
Wenham, 01984

Lesley College
29 Everett Street
Cambridge, 02138-2790

Simmons College
300 The Fenway
Boston, 02115

Tufts University
Medford, 02155

Westfield State College
Western Avenue
Westfield, 01086

Wheelock College
200 The Riverway
Boston, 02215

Michigan

Andrews University
Berrien Springs, 49104

Aquinas College
1607 Robinson Road SE
Grand Rapids, 49506-1799

Calvin College
Grand Rapids, 49506

Central Michigan University
100 Warriner Hall
Mount Pleasant, 48859

Eastern Michigan University
400 Pierce Hall
Silanti, 48197

Grand Valley State University
1 Seidman House
Allendale, 49401-9401

Hope College
Holland, 49423

Madonna University
36600 Schoolcraft Road
Livonia, 48150

Marygrove College
8425 West McNichols Road
Detroit, 48221

Michigan State University
Administration
Building-Room 250
East Lansing, 48824

Northern Michigan University
Cohodas Administration
Center
Marquette, 49855

University of Detroit-Mercy
4001 West McNichols Road
Detroit, 48221

University of Michigan-
Ann Arbor
515 East Jefferson
Room 1220
Ann Arbor, 48109

Wayne State University
  Detroit, 48202

Western Michigan University
  Administration Building
  Kalamazoo, 49008

Minnesota

Bemidji State University
  Bemidji, 56601

Moorhead State University
  1104 Seventh Avenue South
  Moorhead, 56560

St. Cloud State University
  Seventh Street and Fourth
    Avenue South
  St. Cloud, 56301

University of Minnesota-
    Duluth
  184 Darland
    Administration Building
  Duluth, 55801

University of Minnesota-
    Twin Cities
  Minneapolis, 55455-0213

Winona State University
  Winona, 55987

Mississippi

Alcorn State University
  P.O. Box 300
  Lorman, 39096

Blue Mountain College
  Blue Mountain, 38610

Delta State University
  P.O. Box 3151
  Cleveland, 38732

Jackson State University
  1325 J. R. Lynch Street
  Jackson, 39217

Mississippi College
  P.O. Box 4203
  Clinton, 39058

Mississippi State University
  Box 5268
  Mississippi State, 39762

Mississippi University for
    Women
  Columbus, 39701

Tougaloo College
  Tougaloo, 39174

University of Mississippi
  Lyceum Building
  University, 38677

University of Southern
Mississippi
Box 5011-Southern Station
Hattiesburg, 39406

William Carey College
Tuscan Avenue
Hattiesburg, 39401

Missouri

Avila College
11901 Wornail Road
Kansas City, 64145

Central Missouri State
University
Warrensburg, 64093

Culver Stockton College
Canton, 63435

Drury College
900 North Benton Avenue
Springfield, 65082

Evangel College
1111 North Glenstone
Springfield, 65802

Fontbonne College
6800 Wydon Boulevard
St. Louis, 63105

Harris Stowe State College
3026 Laclede Avenue
St. Louis, 63103

Lincoln University
820 Chestnut Street
Jefferson City, 65101

Lindenwood College
St. Charles, 63301-4949

Missouri Southern State
College
Newman and Duquesne
Roads
Joplin, 64801

Missouri Valley College
500 East College
Marshall, 65340

Missouri Western State
College
4525 Downs Drive
St. Joseph, 64507

Northwest Missouri State
University
Maryville, 64468

Southeast Missouri State
University
One University Plaza
Cape Girardeau, 63701

Southwest Missouri State
University
901 South National
Springfield, 65804

St. Louis University
   221 North Grand Boulevard
   St. Louis, 63103

Stephens College
   Columbia, 65215

University of Missouri-
      Columbia
   130 Jesse Hall
   Columbia, 65211

University of Missouri-
      St. Louis
   8001 Natural Bridge Road
   St. Louis, 63121

Webster University
   470 East Lockwood
   St. Louis, 63119

Westminster College
   Seventh and Westminster
      Avenues
   Fulton, 65251

William Woods College
   Fulton, 65251

Montana

Carrol College
   North Benton Avenue
   Helena, 59625

Eastern Montana College
   1500 North Thirtieth Street
   Billings, 59101

Montana State University
   Montana Hall
   Bozeman, 59717

Nebraska

Chadron State College
   Tenth and Main Streets
   Chadron, 69337

College of Saint Mary
   1901 South
      Seventy-second Street
   Omaha, 68124

Concordia College
   800 North Columbia
      Avenue
   Seward, 68434

Creighton University
   California at Twenty-fourth
      Street
   Omaha, 68178

Dana College
   2848 College Drive
   Blair, 68008-1099

Doane College
   Crete, 68333

Hastings College
   Seventh and Turner
      Avenues
   Hastings, 68901

Nebraska Wesleyan
 University
 5000 St. Paul Avenue
 Lincoln, 68504

Peru State College
 Peru, 68421

University of Nebraska at
 Kearney
 905 West Twenty-fifth
 Street
 Kearney, 68849

University of Nebraska-
 Lincoln
 Fourteenth and R Streets
 Lincoln, 68588-0415

University of Nebraska-
 Omaha
 Sixtieth and Dodge Streets
 Omaha, 68182

Wayne State College
 200 East Tenth Street
 Wayne, 68787

Nevada

University of Nevada-
 Las Vegas
 4505 Maryland Parkway
 Las Vegas, 89154

University of Nevada-Reno
 Reno, 89557

New Brunswick

University of New Brunswick
 Fredrickton, New
 Brunswick
 Canada E3B 5A3

New Hampshire

Keene State College
 Main Street
 Keene, 03431

Notre Dame College
 2321 Elm Street
 Manchester, 03104

Rivier College
 South Main Street
 Nashua, 03060

University of New Hampshire
 Garrison Avenue-
 Grant House
 Durham, 03824

New Jersey

Centenary College
 400 Jefferson Street
 Hackettstown, 07840

College of Saint Elizabeth
 Madison Avenue
 Convent Station, 07961

Felician College
260 South Main Street
Lodi, 07644

Georgian Court College
900 Lakewood Avenue
Lakewood, 08701

Glassboro State College
Glassboro, 08028

Jersey City State College
2039 Kennedy Boulevard
Jersey City, 07305

Kean College of New Jersey
Morris Avenue
Union, 07083

Monmouth College
Cedar Avenue
West Long Branch, 07764

Rutgers-The State University
of New Jersey
Douglass College
P.O. Box 2101
New Brunswick, 08903

Rutgers-The State University
of New Jersey
Livingston College
P.O. Box 2101
New Brunswick, 08903

Rutgers-The State University
of New Jersey
Rutgers College
P.O. Box 2101
New Brunswick, 08903

Seton Hall University
400 South Orange Avenue
South Orange, 07079

Trenton State College
Hillwood Lakes CN 4700
Trenton, 08650-4700

William Patterson College
300 Pompton Road
Wayne, 07470

New Mexico

College of the Southwest
6610 Lovington Highway
Hobbs, 88240

Eastern New Mexico
University
Station Seven
Portales, 88130

New Mexico State University
Box 30001-Department 3A
Las Cruces, 88003-0001

University of New Mexico
Albuquerque, 87131

Western New Mexico
   University
   P.O. Box 680
   Silver City, 88061

New York

Adelphi University
   South Avenue
   Garden City, 11530

CUNY-Baruch College
   17 Lexington Avenue
   New York, 10010

CUNY-Brooklyn College
   Bedford Avenue and
      Avenue H
   Brooklyn, 11210

CUNY-City College
   Convent Avenue at 138th
      Street
   New York, 10031

CUNY-College of Staten
      Island
   715 Ocean Terrace
   Staten Island, 10301

CUNY-Lehman College
   Bedford Park Boulevard
      West
   Bronx, 10468

CUNY-Medgar Evers College
   1615 Bedford Avenue
   Brooklyn, 11225-2201

CUNY-York College
   94-20 Guy R. Brewer
      Boulevard
   Jamaica, 11451

College of Mount Saint
      Vincent
   263rd Street and Riverdale
      Avenue
   New York, 10471

College of New Rochelle
   College of Arts and
      Sciences and School of
      Nursing
   Castle Place
   New Rochelle, 10805

College of Saint Rose
   432 Western Avenue
   Albany, 12203

D'Yourville College
   320 Porter Avenue
   Buffalo, 14201

Daemen College
   4380 Main Street
   Amhurst, 14226

Dominican College of
      Blauvelt
   10 Western Highway
   Orangeburg, 10962

Dowling College
  Idle Hour Boulevard
  Oakdale, 11769

Hobart and William Smith
    Colleges
  Geneva, 14456

Iona College
  715 North Avenue
  New Rochelle, 10801

Keuka College
  Keuka Park, 14478

LeMoyne College
  Syracuse, 13214-1399

Long Island University-
    C. W. Post Campus
  Northern Boulevard-
    College Hall
  Greenvale, 11548

Manhattan College
  Manhattan College Parkway
  Riverdale, 10471

Marist College
  North Road
  Poughkeepsie, 12601

Marymount College
  Tarrytown, 10591

Marymount Manhattan
    College
  221 East Seventy-first
    Street
  New York, 10021

Mercy College
  555 Broadway
  Dobbs Ferry, 10522

Molloy College
  1000 Hempstead Avenue
  Rockville Center, 11570

Mount Saint Mary College
  330 Powell Avenue
  Newburgh, 12550

Nazareth College of
    Rochester
  4245 East Avenue
  Rochester, 14610

New York University
  22 Washington Square
    North
  New York, 10011

Russel Sage College
  51 First Street
  Troy, 12180

SUNY-College at Buffalo
  1300 Elmwood Avenue
  Buffalo, 14222

SUNY-College at Fredonia
  Fredonia, 14063

SUNY-College at Geneseo
  Erwin Administration
    Building
  Geneseo, 14454-1471

SUNY-College at New Paltz
  75 South Manheim
    Boulevard
  New Paltz, 12561-2499

SUNY-College at Old
    Westbury
  P.O. Box 307
  Old Westbury, 11568

SUNY-College at Plattsburgh
  Plattsburgh, 12901

Saint John's University
  Grand Central and Utopia
    Parkways
  Jamaica, 11439

Saint Joseph's College
  245 Clinton Avenue
  Brooklyn, 11205

Saint Joseph's College-
    Suffolk
  155 Roe Boulevard
  Patchogue, 11772

Saint Thomas Aquinas
    College
  Route 340
  Sparkill, 10968

Syracuse University
  200 Administration
    Building
  Syracuse, 13244

Vassar College
  Raymond Avenue
  Poughkeepsie, 12601

Wagner College
  631 Howard Avenue
  Staten Island, 10301

North Carolina

Appalachian State University
  Boone, 29608

Belmont Abbey College
  Belmont, 28012

Bennett College
  900 East Washington Street
  Greensboro, 27401

Catawba College
  2300 West Innes Street
  Salisbury, 28144

East Carolina University
  Greenville, 27834

Elizabeth City State
    University
  Parkview Drive
  Elizabeth City, 27909

Greensboro College
815 West Market Street
Greensboro, 27410

High Point University
University Station-
Montlieu Avenue
High Point, 27262-3598

Lenoir-Rhyne College
Box 7227
Hickory, 28603

Livingstone College
701 West Monroe Street
Salisbury, 28114

Methodist College
5400 Ramsay Street
Fayetteville, 28311-1499

Pembroke State University
Pembroke, 28372

Salem College
P.O. Box 10548
Winston-Salem, 27108

Shaw University
118 East South Street
Raleigh, 27611

St. Augustine's College
1315 Oak Avenue
Raleigh, 27610-2298

University of North
Carolina-Asheville
One University Heights
Asheville, 28804

University of North
Carolina-Charlotte
University City Boulevard
Charlotte, 28223

University of North
Carolina-Wilmington
601 South College Road
Wilmington, 28403

Western Carolina University
520 H. F. Robinson
Administration Building
Cullowhee, 28723

Winston-Salem State
University
601 Martin Luther King Jr.
Drive
Winston-Salem, 27110

North Dakota

Dickinson State University
Dickinson, 58601

Minot State University
Minot, 58707

University of Mary
7500 University Drive
Bismarck, 58504

University of North Dakota
    Grank Forks, 58202

Nova Scotia

University College of Cape
        Breton
    P.O. Box 5300
    Sidney, Nova Scotia
    Canada B1P 6L2

University of Kings College
    Halifax, Nova Scotia
    Canada B3H 2A1

Ohio

Ashland University
    College Avenue
    Ashland, 44805

Baldwin-Wallace College
    275 Eastland Road
    Berea, 44017

Bluffton College
    Box 638-Marbeck Center
    Bluffton, 45817

Bowling Green State
        University
    110 McFall Center
    Bowling Green, 43403

Cedarville College
    Box 601
    Cedarville, 45314

Central State University
    Brush Row Road
    Wilberforce, 45384

Cleveland State University
    East Twenty-fourth and
        Euclid Avenues
    Cleveland, 44115

College of Mount Saint
        Joseph
    5701 Delhi Road
    Cincinnati, 45233-9314

The Defiance College
    701 North Clinton Street
    Defiance, 43512

Franciscan University of
        Stuebenville
    Franciscan Way
    Stuebenville, 43952

Heidelberg College
    310 East Market Street
    Tiffin, 44883

Hiram College
    P.O. Box 96
    Hiram, 44234

Kent State University
    P.O. Box 5190
    Kent, 44242-0001

Malone College
    515 Twenty-fifth Street NW
    Canton, 44708

Miami University
Oxford, 45056

Mount Union College
1972 Clark Avenue
Alliance, 44601

Mount Vernon Nazarene
College
800 Martinsburg Road
Mount Vernon, 43050

Muskingum College
New Concord, 43762

Notre Dame College of Ohio
4545 College Road
Cleveland, 44121

Ohio Dominican College
1216 Sunbury Road
Columbus, 43219

Ohio Northern University
Main Street
Ada, 45810

Ohio State University-
Columbus
1800 Cannon Drive-
1210 Lincoln Tower
Columbus, 43210

Ohio University
120 Chubb Hall
Athens, 45701

University of Akron
381 East Buchtel Commons
Akron, 44325-2001

University of Cincinnati
100 French Hall
Cincinnati, 45221

University of Dayton
300 College Park
Dayton, 45469

University of Findlay
1000 North Main Street
Findlay, 45840

University of Rio Grande
P.O. Box 909
Rio Grande, 45674

University of Toledo
2801 West Bancroft Street
Toledo, 43606

Urbana University
579 College Way
Urbana, 43078-2091

Ursuline College
2550 Lander Road
Pepper Pike, 44124

Walsh College
2020 Easton Street NW
North Canton, 44720

Wittenburg University
P.O. Box 720
Springfield, 45501

Wright State University
  Colonel Glenn Highway
  Dayton, 45435

Xavier University
  3800 Victory Parkway
  Cincinnati, 45207

Youngstown State University
  Youngstown, 44555

Oklahoma

Cameron University
  2800 Gore Boulevard
  Lawton, 73505

East Central University
  Ada, 74820-6899

Northeastern State University
  Tahlequah, 74464

Northwestern State University
  709 Oklahoma Boulevard
  Alva, 73717

Oklahoma State University
  103 Whitehurst Hall
  Stillwater, 74078

Southwestern Oklahoma
  State University
  Weatherford, 73096

University of Central
  Oklahoma
  Edmond, 73034-0172

University of Oklahoma-
  Norman
  1000 Asp Avenue
  Norman, 73019

University of Science and
  Arts of Oklahoma
  Seventeenth Street and
  Grand Avenue
  Chickasha, 73018

Ontario

University of Ottawa
  Ottawa, Ontario
  Canada K1N 6N5

University of Toronto
  Toronto, Ontario
  Canada M5S 1A1

University of Waterloo
  Waterloo, Ontario
  Canada N2L 3G1

University of Western Ontario
  London, Ontario
  Canada N6B 3P4

University of Windsor
  Windsor, Ontario
  Canada N9B 3P4

Oregon

University of Oregon
  240 Oregon Hall
  Eugene, 97403

University of Portland
  5000 North Willamette
    Boulevard
  Portland, 97203

Warner Pacific College
  2219 Southeast
    Sixty-eighth Street
  Portland, 97215

Western Oregon State College
  Monmouth, 97361

Pennsylvania

Beaver College
  Church and Easton Roads
  Glenside, 19038

Bloomsburg University of
    Pennsylvania
  Ben Franklin Building
  Bloomsburg, 17815

Cabrini College
  610 King of Prussia Road
  Radnor, 19087-3699

California University of
    Pennsylvania
  250 University Avenue
  California, 15419-1394

Carlow College
  3333 Fifth Avenue
  Pittsburgh, 15213

Cheyney University of
    Pennsylvania
  Cheyney, 19319

Clarion University of
    Pennsylvania
  Clarion, 16214

College Misericordia
  Lake Street
  Dalla, 18612

Duquesne University
  600 Forbes Avenue
  Pittsburgh, 15282

East Stroudsburg University
    of Pennsylvania
  East Stroudsburg, 18301

Edinboro University of
    Pennsylvania
  Edinboro, 16444

Gannon University
  University Square
  Erie, 16541

Gannon University-Villa
    Marie Campus
  2551 West Lake Road
  Erie, 16505

Gwynedd-Mercy College
  Sumneytown Pike
  Gwynedd Valley, 19437

Holy Family College
  Grant and Frankford
    Avenues
  Philadelphia, 19114

Indiana University of
    Pennsylvania
  Indiana, 15705

King's College
  133 North River Street
  Wilkes-Barre, 18711

Kutztown University
  College Hill
  Kutztown, 19530

LaSalle University
  Olney Avenue at Twentieth
    Street
  Philadelphia, 19141

Lincoln University
  Lincoln Hall
  Lincoln University, 19352

Lock Haven University of
    Pennsylvania
  Lock Haven, 17745

Mansfield University of
    Pennsylvania
  Alumni Hall
  Mansfield, 16933

Marywood College
  2300 Adams Avenue
  Scranton, 18509

Mercyhurst College
  Glenwood Hills
  Erie, 16546

Millersville University of
    Pennsylvania
  P.O. Box 1002
  Millersville, 175521-0302

Penn State-University Park
  201 Shields Building
  University Park, 16802

Slippery Rock University of
    Pennsylvania
  Slippery Rock, 16057

Temple University
  Philadelphia, 19122

Villanova University
  Villanova, 19085

West Chester University of
    Pennsylvania
  West Chester, 19383

Prince Edward Island

University of Prince Edward
    Island
  550 University Avenue
  Charlottetown, Prince
    Edward Island
  Canada C1A 4B3

Puerto Rico

American University of
Puerto Rico
P.O. Box 2037
Bayamon, Puerto Rico
00621

Inter-American University of
Puerto Rico
Arecibo Campus
Call Box UI
Arecibo, Puerto Rico 00613

Pontifical Catholic
University of Puerto Rico
Las Americas Avenue-
Station Six
Ponce, Puerto Rico 00731

University of Puerto Rico
Rio Piedras Campus
P.O. Box 22334 UPR
Station
Rio Piedras, Puerto Rico
00931

Rhode Island

Providence College
River Avenue
Providence, 02918

Rhode Island College
Providence, 02908

Salve Regina University
Ochre Point Avenue
Newport, 02840-4192

Saskatchewan

University of Regina
Regina, Saskatchewan
Canada S4S 0A2

University of Saskatchewan
Saskatoon, Saskatchewan
Canada S7N 0W8

South Carolina

Central Wesleyan College
Central, 29630

Coker College
College Avenue
Hartsville, 29550

College of Charleston
Sixty-six George Street
Charleston, 29424

Columbia College
1301 Columbia College
Drive
Columbia, 29203

Converse College
580 East Main Street
Spartanburg, 29301

Erskine College
Due West, 29639

Furman University
  3200 Poinsett Highway
  Greenville, 29613-0645

Lander University
  Stanley Avenue
  Greenwood, 29649

Presbyterian College
  Broad Street
  Clinton, 29325

South Carolina State
    University
  Orangeburg, 29117-0001

Winthrop University
  Oakland Avenue
  Rock Hill, 29733

South Dakota

Augustana College
  Twenty-ninth and Summit
    Avenue
  Sioux Falls, 57197

Black Hills State University
  1200 University Street
  Spearfish, 57783

Dakota State University
  Heston Hall
  Madison, 57042

Northern State University
  Aberdeen, 57401

Sioux Falls College
  1501 South Prairie Street
  Sioux Falls, 57105

University of South Dakota
  414 East Clark
  Vermillion, 57069

Tennessee

Auston Peay State University
  P.O. Box 4548
  Clarksville, 37040

Belmont University
  1900 Belmont Boulevard
  Nashville, 37212

Bryan College
  Box 7000
  Dayton, 37321

Carson-Newman College
  Russell Avenue
  Jefferson City, 37760

East Tennessee State
    University
  Campus Box 244030-A
  Johnson City, 37614

Freed-Hardeman University
  158 East Main Street
  Henderson, 38340

Lambuth College
  Lambuth Boulevard
  Jackson, 38301

Memphis State University
  Memphis, 38152

Middle Tennessee State
  University
  Murfreesboro, 37132

Tennessee State University
  3500 John Merritt
  Boulevard
  Nashville, 37203

Tennessee Technological
  University
  Dixie Avenue
  Cookeville, 38505

Union University
  2447 Highway 45 By-Pass
  Jackson, 38305

University of Tennessee-
  Chattanooga
  McCallie Avenue-
  129 Hooper Hall
  Chattanooga, 37403

University of Tennessee-
  Knoxville
  320 Student Services
  Building
  Knoxville, 37996-0230

University of Tennessee-
  Martin
  Martin, 38238

Vanderbilt University
  2305 West End Avenue
  Nashville, 37203

Texas

Angelo State University
  2601 West Avenue N
  San Angelo, 76909

Baylor University
  P.O. Box 97008
  Waco, 76798-7008

Corpus Christi State
  University
  6300 Ocean Drive
  Corpus Christi, 78412

East Texas State University
  East Texas Station
  Commerce, 75429

Incarnate Word College
  4301 Broadway
  San Antonio, 78209

Lamar University
  P.O. Box 10009
  Beaumont, 77710

Laredo State University
  One West End Washington
  Street
  Laredo, 78040-0960

Midwestern State University
   3400 Taft Boulevard
   Wichita Falls, 76308

Our Lady of the Lake-
      University of San
      Antonio
   411 Southwest
      Twenty-fourth Street
   San Antonio, 78207-4689

Prairie View A and M
      University
   P.O. Box 2610
   Prairie View, 77446

Sam Houston State University
   Huntsville, 77341

Southwest Texas State
      University
   J. C. Kellam Building
   San Marcos, 78666

Stephen F. Austin State
      University
   Nacogdoches, 75962

Texas Southern University
   3100 Cleburne
   Houston, 77004

Texas Technical University
   P.O. Box 42017
   Lubbock, 79409

Texas Women's University
   P.O. Box 22909-
      TWU Station
   Denton, 76204

University of Houston-
      Clear Lake
   2700 Bay Area Boulevard
   Houston, 77058

University of Mary Hardin-
      Baylor
   P.O. Box 403
   Belton, 76513

University of Saint Thomas
   3812 Montrose
   Houston, 77006

University of Texas-Austin
   Austin, 78712

University of Texas-El Paso
   El Paso, 79968

University of Texas-
      Permian Basin
   Box 8422-UTPB
   Odessa, 79762

University of Texas-Tyler
   3900 University Boulevard
   Tyler, 75701

West Texas State University
   Canyon, 79016

Utah

University of Utah
  250 Student Services
    Building
  Salt Lake City, 84112

Utah State University
  Logan, 84322

Vermont

Castleton State College
  Castleton, 05735

College of Saint Joseph in
    Vermont
  Clement Road-St. Joseph
    Hall
  Rutland, 05701

Green Mountain College
  16 College Street
  Poultney, 05764

Johnson State College
  Stowe Road
  Johnson, 05656

Lyndon State College
  Lyndonville, 05851

Trinity College
  208 Colechester Avenue
  Burlington, 05401

University of Vermont
  194 South Prospect Street
  Burlington, 05401-3596

Virginia

Eastern Mennonite College
  Harrisburg, 22801

Hampton University
  Hampton, 23668

James Madison University
  Harrisonburg, 22807

Longwood College
  Farmville, 23909

Lynchburg College
  1501 Lakeside Drive
  Lynchburg, 24501

Mary Baldwin College
  Staunton, 24401

Norfolk State University
  2401 Corprew Avenue
  Norfolk, 23529-0050

Old Dominion University
  Hampton Boulevard
  Norfolk, 23529-0050

Radford University
  Radford, 24142

Virginia Commonwealth
University
P.O. Box 2526-821 West
Franklin Street
Richmond, 23284-2526

Virginia State University
Box 9018
Petersburg, 23806

Virginia Union University
1500 North Lombardy
Street
Richmond, 23220

Washington

Central Washington
University
Mitchell Hall
Ellensburg, 98926

Eastern Washington
University
Showalter Hall-Room 117
Cheney, 99004

Gonzaga University
Spokane, 99258

Saint Martin's College
5300 Pacific Avenue SE
Lacey, 98503-1297

Seattle Pacific University
3307 Third Avenue West
Seattle, 98119

Washington State University
342 French Administration
Building
Pullman, 99164

Western Washington
University
Old Main-Room 200
Bellingham, 98225

Whitworth College
Spokane, 99251

West Virginia

Alderson-Broadus College
Phillippi, 26416

Bethany College
Bethany, 26032

Bluefield State College
Bluefield, 24701

Concord College
Athens, 24712

Fairmont State College
Locust Avenue Extension
Fairmont, 26554

Glenville State College
Glenville, 26351

Marshall University
400 Hal Greer Boulevard
Huntington, 25755

West Liberty State College
West Liberty, 26074

West Virginia University
P.O. Box 6009
Morgantown, 26506-6009

Wisconsin

Cardinal Stritch College
6801 North Yates Road
Milwaukee, 53217

Carthage College
2001 Alford Park Drive
Kenosha, 53140-1994

Edgewood College
855 Woodrow Street
Madison, 53711

Siler Lake College
2406 South Alverno Road
Manitowoc, 54220

University of Wisconsin-
Eau Claire
Eau Claire, 54701

University of Wisconsin-
Milwaukee
P.O. Box 749
Milwaukee, 53201

University of Wisconsin-
Oshkosh
135 Dempsey Hall
Oshkosh, 54901

University of Wisconsin-
Stevens Point
Stevens Point, 54481

University of Wisconsin-
Whitewater
800 West Main Street
Whitewater, 53190

Wyoming

University of Wyoming
Box 3435-University
Station
Laramie, 82071

PROGRAMS FOR COMMUNICATION DISORDERS

Following is an alphabetical list of American colleges and universities that specialize in various programs for communication disorders:

Alabama

Alabama A and M University
  P.O. Box 384
  Normal, 35762

Auburn University
  Mary E. Martin Hall
  Auburn University, 36849

University of Alabama
  Box 870132
  Tuscaloosa, 35487-0132

University of Montevallo
  Montevallo, 35115

University of South Alabama
  307 University Boulevard
  Mobile, 36688

Arizona

Arizona State University
  Tempe, 85287-0112

Northern Arizona University
  Box 4084
  Flagstaff, 86011

University of Arizona
  Tucson, 85721

Arkansas

Arkansas State University
  P.O. Box 1630
  State University, 72467

Harding University
  Box 762-Station A
  Searcy, 72143

Henderson State University
  Arkadelphia, 71923

University of Arkansas
  Administration 222
  Fayetteville, 72701

University of Arkansas-
    Little Rock
  2801 South University
  Little Rock, 72204

University of Central
    Arkansas
  Conway, 72032

California

California State University-
    Chico
  Chico, 95929

California State University-
    Fresno
  Shaw and Cedar Avenues
  Fresno, 93740

California State University-
    Hayward
  Hayward, 94542

California State University-
    Long Beach
  1250 Bellflower Boulevard
  Long Beach, 90840

California State University-
    Northridge
  18111 Nordhoff Street
  Northridge, 91330

California State University-
    Sacramento
  6000 J Street
  Sacramento, 95819

Humboldt State University
  Arcato, 95521

Point Loma Nazarene College
  3900 Lomaland Drive
  San Diego, 92106

San Diego State University
  5300 Campanile Drive
  San Diego, 92182

San Francisco State
    University
  1600 Holloway Avenue
  San Francisco, 94132

San Jose State University
  One Washington Square
  San Jose, 95192-0009

University of California-
Santa Barbara
1210 Cheadle Hall
Santa Barbara, 93106

University of the Pacific
3601 Pacific Avenue
Stockton, 95211

University of Redlands
P.O. Box 3080
Redlands, 92373-0999

Whittier College
13406 East Philadelphia
Whittier, 90608

Colorado

University of Colorado-
Boulder
Campus Box B-7
Boulder, 80309

University of Northern
Colorado
Greeley, 80639

Connecticut

Southern Connecticut State
University
501 Crescent Street
New Haven, 06515

District of Columbia

University of the District of
Columbia
4200 Connecticut Avenue
NW
Washington, DC 20008

Florida

Florida State University
Tallahassee, 32306

University of Central Florida
P.O. Box 25000
Orlando, 32816

University of Florida
135 Tigert Hall
Gainesville, 32611

Georgia

Albany State College
504 College Drive
Albany, 31705

University of Georgia
114 Academic Building
Athens, 30602

Hawaii

University of Hawaii-Manoa
2530 Dole Street-
Room C200
Honolulu, 96822

Idaho

Idaho State University
P.O. Box 8054
Pocatello, 83209

Northwest Nazarene College
Dewey at Holly Street
Nampa, 83686

Illinois

Augustana College
639 Thirty-eighth Street
Rock Island, 61201

Eastern Illinois University
Old Main-Room 116
Charleston, 61902

Elmhurst College
190 Prospect Avenue
Elmhurst, 60126-3296

Governors State University
University Parkway
University Park, 60466

Illinois State University
201 Hovey Hall
Normal, 61761

Northern Illinois University
DeKalb, 60115

Northwestern University
P.O. Box 3060-
1801 Hinman Avenue
Evanston, 60201-3060

Southern Illinois University
at Carbondale
Woody Hall
Carbondale, 62901

Southern Illinois University
at Edwardsville
Box 1047
Edwardsville, 62026

Saint Xavier University
3700 West One Hundred
and Third Street
Chicago, 60655

University of Illinois at
Urbana-Champaign
506 South Wright Street
Urbana, 60801

Western Illinois University
900 West Adams Street
Macomb, 61455-1383

Indiana

Ball State University
2000 University Avenue
Muncie, 47306

Butler University
  Forty-sixth and Sunset
    Avenue
  Indianapolis, 46208

Indiana State University
  217 North Sixth Street
  Terre Haute, 47809

Indiana University-
    Bloomington
  814 East Third Street
  Bloomington, 47405

Purdue University
  Schleman Hall
  West Lafayette, 47907

Valparaiso University
  Valparaiso, 46383

Iowa

University of Iowa
  108 Calvin Hall
  Iowa City, 52242

University of Northern Iowa
  West Twenty-seventh Street
  Cedar Falls, 50614

Kansas

Fort Hays State University
  600 Park Street
  Hays, 67601

Kansas State University
  Anderson Hall
  Manhattan, 66506

University of Kansas
  126 Strong Hall
  Lawrence, 66045

Wichita State University
  8545 Fairmount Street
  Wichita, 67208

Kentucky

Brescia College
  717 Frederica Street
  Owensboro, 42301

Eastern Kentucky University
  Lancaster Avenue
  Richmond, 40475

Murray State University
  Murray, 42071

University of Kentucky
  100 Funkhouser Avenue
  Lexington, 40506

Western Kentucky University
  Wetherby Administration
    Building-Room 209
  Bowling Green, 40506

Louisiana

Grambling State University
  Grambling, 71245

Louisiana State University-
   Shreveport
One University Place
Shreveport, 71115

Louisiana State University
   and Agricultural and
   Mechanical College
110 Thomas Boyd Hall
Baton Rouge, 70803

Louisiana Technical
   University
P.O. Box 3168 Tech Station
Ruston, 71272

Nicholls State University
P.O. Box 2004-
   University Station
Thibodaux, 70310

Northeast Louisiana
   University
700 University Avenue
Monroe, 71209

Southern University-
   Baton Rouge
P.O. Box 901-
   Southern Branch
Baton Rouge, 70813

Southern University at New
   Orleans
6400 Press Drive
New Orleans, 70126

University of Southwest
   Louisiana
P.O. Box 41770
Lafayette, 70504

Xavier University of
   Louisiana
7325 Palmetto Street
New Orleans, 70125

Maine

University of Maine at
   Farmington
102 Main Street
Farmington, 04938

Maryland

Loyola College
4501 North Charles Street
Baltimore, 21210

University of Maryland at
   College Park
College Park, 20742

Massachusetts

Boston University
121 Bay State Road
Boston, 02215

Bridgewater State College
Bridgewater, 02325

Elms College
291 Springfield Street
Chicopee, 01013-2839

Emerson College
100 Beacon Street
Boston, 02116

University of Massachusetts-
Amherst
University Admissions
Center
Amherst, 01003

Worcester State College
486 Chandler Street
Worcester, 01602-2597

Michigan

Andrews University
Berrien Springs, 49104

Central Michigan University
100 Warriner Hall
Mount Pleasant, 48859

Eastern Michigan University
400 Pierce Hall
Silanti, 48197

Michigan State University
Administation
Building-Room 250
East Lansing, 48824

Northern Michigan University
Cohodas Administration
Center
Marquette, 49055

Wayne State University
Detroit, 48202

Western Michigan University
Administration Building
Kalamazoo, 49008

Minnesota

Mankato State University
Box 55
Mankato, 56001

Moorhead State University
1104 Seventh Avenue South
Moorhead, 56560

Saint Cloud State University
Seventh Street and Fourth
Avenue South
Saint Cloud, 56301

University of Minnesota-
Duluth
184 Darland
Administration Building
Duluth, 55812

University of Minnesota-
Twin Cities
Minneapolis, 55455-0213

Mississippi

Jackson State University
1325 J. R. Lynch Street
Jackson, 39217

Mississippi College
P.O. Box 4203
Clinton, 39058

Mississippi University for
Women
Columbus, 39701

University of Mississippi
Lyceum Building
University, 38677

University of Southern
Mississippi
Box 5011-Southern Station
Hattiesburg, 39406

Missouri

Central Missouri State
University
6800 Wydown Boulevard
St. Louis, 63105

Fontbonne College
6800 Wydown Boulevard
St. Louis, 63105

Northeast Missouri State
University
A/H 205
Kirksville, 63501

Southeast Missouri State
University
One University Plaza
Cape Girardeau, 63701

Southwest Missouri State
University
901 South National
Springfield, 65804

St. Louis University
221 North Grand Boulevard
St. Louis, 63102

University of Missouri-
Columbia
130 Jesse Hall
Columbia, 65211

Washington University
Campus Box 1089
St. Louis, 63130

Montana

University of Montana
Lodge 101
Missoula, 59812

Nebraska

University of Nebraska at
Kearney
905 West Twenty-fifth
Street
Kearney, 68849

University of Nebraska-
   Lincoln
Fourteenth and R Streets
Lincoln, 68588-0415

Nevada

University of Nevada-Reno
   Reno, 89557

New Hampshire

University of New Hampshire
   Garrison Avenue-
      Grant House
   Durham, 03824

New Jersey   ·

Kean College of New Jersey
   Montclair State College
   Valley Road and Normal
      Avenue
   Upper Montclair,
      07043-1624

Rutgers-The State University
   of New Jersey
   Douglass College
   P.O. Box 2101
   New Brunswick, 08903

Rutgers-The State University
   of New Jersey
   Livingston College
   P.O. Box 2101
   New Brunswick, 08903

Rutgers-The State University
   of New Jersey
   Rutgers College
   P.O. Box 2101
   New Brunswick, 08903

Rutgers-The State University
   of New Jersey
   University College-
      New Brunswick
   14 College Avenue
   New Brunswick, 08903

Stockton State College
   Pomona, 08240

Trenton State College
   Hillwood Lakes CN 4700
   Trenton, 08650-4700

William Patterson College
   300 Pompton Road
   Wayne, 07470

New Mexico

Eastern New Mexico
   University
   Station Seven
   Portales, 88130

New Mexico State University
   Box 30001 Department 3A
   Las Cruces, 88003-0001

University of New Mexico
   Albuquerque, 87131

New York

Adelphi University
South Avenue
Garden City, 11530

CUNY Brooklyn College
Bedford Avenue and
Avenue H
Brooklyn, 11210

CUNY-Lehman College
Bedford Park Boulevard
West
Bronx, 10468

CUNY-Queens College
65-30 Kissena Boulevard
Flushing, 11367

College of Saint Rose
432 Western Avenue
Albany, 12203

Elmira College
Park Place
Elmira, 14901

Hofstra University
Hempstead, 11550

Iona College
715 North Avenue
New Rochelle, 10801

Ithaca College
Ithaca, 14850

Long Island University-
Brooklyn Campus
University Plaza
Brooklyn, 11201

Long Island University-
C.W. Post Campus
Northern Boulevard-
College Hall
Greenvale, 11548

Marymount Manhattan
College
221 East Seventy-first
Street
New York, 10021

Nazareth College of
Rochester
4245 East Avenue
Rochester, 14610

New York University
22 Washington Square
North
New York, 10011

Pace University
Pace Plaza
New York 10038

SUNY-Buffalo
3435 Main Street
Buffalo, 14214

SUNY-College at Buffalo
1300 Elmwood Avenue
Buffalo, 14222

SUNY-College at Cortland
P.O. Box 2000
Cortland, 13045

SUNY-College at Fredonia
Fredonia, 14063

SUNY-College at Geneseo
Erwin Administration
Building
Geneseo, 14454-1471

SUNY College at New Paltz
Seventy-five South
Manheim Road
New Paltz, 12561-2499

SUNY-College at Plattsburgh
Plattsburgh, 12901

Saint John's University
Grand Central and Utopia
Parkway
Jamaica, 11439

Syracuse University
200 Administration
Building
Syracuse, 13244

North Carolina

Appalachian State University
Boone, 28608

East Carolina University
Greenville, 27834

Shaw University
118 East South Street
Raleigh, 27611

University of North Carolina-
Greensboro
1000 Spring Garden Street
Greensboro, 27412

Western Carolina University
520 H. F. Robinson
Administration Building
Cullowhee, 28723

North Dakota

Minot State University
Minot, 58707

University of North Dakota
Grand Forks, 58202

Ohio

Baldwin-Wallace College
275 Eastland Road
Berea, 44017

Bowling Green State
University
110 McFall Center
Bowling Green, 43403

Case Western Reserve
    University
    Tomlinson Hall
    Cleveland, 44106

Cleveland State University
    East Twenty-fourth and
        Euclid Avenue
    Cleveland, 44115

Kent State University
    P.O. Box 5190
    Kent, 44242-0001

Miami University
    Oxford, 45056

Ohio State University-
        Columbus
    1800 Cannon Drive-
        1210 Lincoln Tower
    Columbus, 43210

Ohio University
    120 Chubb Hall
    Athens, 45701

University of Cincinnati
    100 French Hall
    Cincinatti, 45221

University of Toledo
    2801 West Bancroft Street
    Toledo, 43606

Oklahoma

Northeastern State University
    Tahlequah, 74464

Oklahoma State University
    103 Whitehurst Hall
    Stillwater, 74078

University of Central
        Oklahoma
    Edmond, 73034-0172

University of Oklahoma-
        Health Sciences Center
    P.O. Box 26901
    Oklahoma City, 73190

University of Oklahoma-
        Norman
    100 Asp Avenue
    Norman, 73019

University of Science and
        Arts of Oklahoma
    Seventeenth Street and
        Grand Avenue
    Chickasha, 73018

University of Tulsa
    600 South College Avenue
    Tulsa, 74104

Oregon

Portland State University
    P.O. Box 751
    Portland, 97207-0751

University of Oregon
  240 Oregon Hall
  Eugene, 97403

Pennsylvania

Bloomsburg University of
    Pennsylvania
  Ben Franklin Building
  Bloomsburg, 17815

California University of
    Pennsylvania
  250 University Avenue
  California, 15419-1394

Clarion University of
    Pennsylvania
  Clarion, 16214

East Stroudsburg University
    of Pennsylvania
  East Stroudsburg, 18301

Geneva College
  Beaver Falls, 15010

Indiana University of
    Pennsylvania
  Indiana, 15705

Marywood College
  2300 Adams Avenue
  Scranton, 18509

Penn State-University Park
  201 Shields Building
  University Park, 16802

Temple University
  Philadelphia, 19122

West Chester University of
    Pennsylvania
  West Chester, 19383

Rhode Island

University of Rhode Island
  Green Hall
  Kingston, 02881

South Carolina

Columbia College
  1301 Columbia College
    Drive
  Columbia, 29203

South Carolina State
    University
  Orangeburg, 29117-0001

South Dakota

Augustana College
  Twenty-ninth and Summit
    Avenue
  Sioux Falls, 57197

Northern State University
  Aberdeen, 57401

South Dakota State University
  Box 2201-Administration
    Building-Room 200
  Brookings, 57007

University of South Dakota
414 East Clark
Vermillion, 57069

Tennessee

East Tennessee State
University
Campus Box 24430-A
Johnson City, 37614

Lambuth College
Lambuth Boulevard
Jackson, 38301

Tennessee State University
3500 John Merritt
Boulevard
Nashville, 37203

University of Tennessee-
Knoxville
320 Student Services
Building
Knoxville, 37996-0230

Texas

Baylor University
P.O. Box 97008
Waco, 76798-7008

Hardin-Simmons University
Abilene, 79698

Lamar University
P.O. Box 10009
Beaumont, 77710

Our Lady of the Lake
University of San
Antonio
411 Southwest
Twenty-fourth Street
San Antonio, 78207-4689

Southwest Texas State
University
J. C. Kellam Building
San Marcos, 78666

Texas Southern University
3100 Cleburne
Houston, 77004

Texas Tech University
P.O. Box 42017
Lubbock, 79409

Texas Women's University
P.O. Box 22909 TWU
Station
Denton, 76204

University of Houston
4800 Calhoun
Houston, 77294-2161

University of North Texas
Box 13797
Denton, 76203

University of Texas-Dallas
P.O. Box 830688
Richardson, 75083-0688

University of Texas-El Paso
El Paso, 79968

University of Texas-
Pan American
1201 West University Drive
Edinburgh, 78539

Utah

University of Utah
250 Student Services
Building
Salt Lake City, 84112

Utah State University
Logan, 84322

Vermont

University of Vermont
194 South Prospect Street
Burlington, 05401-3596

Virginia

Hampton University
Hampton, 23668

James Madison University
Harrisonburg, 22807

Longwood College
Farmville, 23909

Norfolk State University
2401 Corprew Avenue
Norfolk, 23504

Old Dominion University
Hampton Boulevard
Norfolk, 23529-0050

Radford University
Radford, 24142

University of Virginia
Box 9017-University
Station
Charlottesville, 22906

Washington

Eastern Washington
University
Showalter Hall-Room 117
Cheney, 99004

University of Washington
Seattle, 98195

Walla Walla College
College Place, 99324

Washington State University
342 French Administration
Building
Pullman, 99164

Western Washington
University
Old Main-Room 200
Bellingham, 98225

West Virginia

Marshall University
   400 Hal Greer Boulevard
   Huntington, 25755

West Virginia University
   P.O. Box 6009
   Morgantown, 26506-6009

Wisconsin

University of Wisconsin-
   Eau Claire
   Eau Claire, 54701

University of Wisconsin-
   Madison
   750 University Avenue
   Madison, 53706

University of Wisconsin-
   Milwaukee
   P.O. Box 749
   Milwaukee, 53201

University of Wisconsin-
   Oshkosh
   135 Dempsey Hall
   Oshkosh, 54901

University of Wisconsin-
   River Falls
   Hawthorne Cottage
   River Falls, 54022

University of Wisconsin-
   Stevens Point
   Stevens Point, 54481

University of Wisconsin-
   Whitewater
   800 West Main Street
   Whitewater, 53190

Wyoming

University of Wyoming
   Box 3435-University
   Station
   Laramie, 82071

EDUCATION PROGRAMS FOR STUDENTS WITH HANDICAPS

Following is an alphabetical list of American universities that offer education programs for students with handicaps:

Alabama

Auburn University
Mary E. Martin Hall
Auburn University, 36849

Talladega College
637 West Battle Street
Talladega, 35160

University of South Alabama
307 University Boulevard
Mobile, 36688

Arkansas

University of Central
Arkansas
Conway, 72032

California

California State University-
Northridge
18111 Nordhoff Street
Northridge, 91330

San Diego State University
5300 Campanile Avenue
San Diego, 92182

San Francisco State
University
1600 Holloway Avenue
San Francisco, 94132

University of the Pacific
3601 Pacific Avenue
Stockton, 95211

Colorado

University of Northern
   Colorado
Greeley, 80639

Florida

Flagler College
P.O. Box 1027
St. Augustine, 32085

Florida State University
Tallahassee, 32306

Illinois

MacMurray College
447 East College Street
Jacksonville, 62650

Indiana

Indiana State University
217 North Sixth Street
Terre Haute, 47809

Iowa

Morningside College
1501 Morningside Avenue
Sioux City, 51106

Kansas

Fort Hays State University
600 Park Street
Hays, 67601

Wichita State University
1845 Fairmount Street
Wichita, 67208

Kentucky

Eastern Kentucky University
Lancaster Avenue
Richmond, 40475

University of Louisville
Louisville, 40292

Louisiana

Louisiana Tech University
P.O. Box 3168 Tech Station
Shreveport, 71115

Southern University-
   Baton Rouge
P.O. Box 9901-
   Southern Branch
Baton Rouge, 70813

Massachusetts

Boston University
121 Bay State Road
Boston, 02215

Michigan

Eastern Michigan University
400 Pierce Hall
Silanti, 48197

Grand Valley State University
1 Seidman House
Allendale, 49401-9401

Western Michigan University
Administration Building
Kalamazoo, 49008

Mississippi

Jackson State University
1325 J. R. Lynch Street
Jackson, 39217

Mississippi College
P.O. Box 4203
Clinton, 39058

University of Southern
Mississippi
Box 5011-Southern Station
Hattiesburg, 39406

Missouri

Fontbonne College
6800 Wydown Boulevard
St. Louis, 63105

Lindenwood College
St. Charles, 63301-4949

Southeast Missouri State
University
One University Plaza
Cape Girardeau, 63701

Nebraska

Nebraska Wesleyan
University
6000 St. Paul Avenue
Lincoln, 68504

University of Nebraska-
Lincoln
Fourteenth and R Streets
Lincoln, 68588-0415

University of Nebraska-
Omaha
Sixtieth and Dodge Streets
Omaha, 68182

New Jersey

Felician College
260 South Main Street
Lodi, 07644

Kean College of New Jersey
Morris Avenue
Union, 07083

Trenton State College
Hillwood Lakes CN 4700
Trenton, 98650-4700

New York

Dominican College of
Blauvelt
10 Western Highway
Orangeburg, 10962

D'Yourville College
320 Porter Avenue
Buffalo, 14201

Iona College
715 North Avenue
Ithaca, 14850

Long Island University-
C.W. Post Campus
Northern Boulevard-
College Hall
Greenvale, 11548

Marymount Manhattan
College
221 East Seventy-first
Street
Manhattan, 10021

New York University
22 Washington Square
North
New York, 10011

SUNY-College at Buffalo
1300 Elmwood Avenue
Buffalo, 14222

SUNY-College at Geneseo
Erwin Administration
Building
Geneseo, 14454-1471

North Carolina

Barton College
College Station
Wilson, 27893

Lenoir-Rhyne College
Box 722
Hickory, 28603

University of North
Carolina-Greensboro
1000 Spring Garden Street
Greensboro, 27412

North Dakota

Minot State University
Minot, 58707

Ohio

Bowling Green State
University
110 McFall Center
Bowling Green, 43403

Cleveland State University
East Twenty-fourth and
Euclid Avenue
Cleveland, 44115

University of Akron
381 East Buchtel Commons
Akron, 44325-2001

University of Toledo
2801 West Bancroft Street
Toledo, 43606

Wright State University
Colonel Glenn Highway
Dayton, 45435

Oklahoma

University of Central
Oklahoma
Edmond, 73034-0172

University of Science and
Arts of Oklahoma
Seventeenth Street and
Grand Avenue
Chickasha, 73018

Oregon

Lewis and Clark College
Portland, 97219

Western Oregon State
University
Monmouth, 97361

Pennsylvania

California University of
Pennsylvania
250 University Avenue
California, 15419-1394

Duquesne University
600 Forbes Avenue
Pittsburgh, 15282

Edinboro University of
Pennsylvania
Edinboro, 16444

Gwynedd-Mercy College
Sumneytown Pike
Gwynedd, 19437

Indiana University of
Pennsylvania
Indiana, 15705

Kutztown University
College Hill
Kutztown, 19530

Mercyhust College
Glenwood Hills
Erie, 16546

Slippery Rock University of
Pennsylvania
Slippery Rock, 16057

Puerto Rico

University of Puerto Rico
Rio Piedras Campus
P.O. Box 22334 UPR
Station
Rio Piedras, Puerto Rico
00931

South Carolina

Converse College
  580 East Main Street
  Spartanburg, 29301

South Dakota

Augustana College
  Twenty-ninth and Summit
    Avenue
  Sioux Falls, 57197

Northern State University
  Aberdeen, 57401

Tennessee

Vanderbilt University
  2305 West End Avenue
  Nashville, 37203

Texas

East Texas State University
  East Texas Station
  Commerce, 75429

Lamar University
  P.O. Box 10009
  Beaumont, 77710

Stephen F. Austin State
  University
  Nacogdoches, 75962

Texas Tech University
  P.O. Box 42017
  Lubbock, 79409

Texas Women's University
  P.O. Box 22909-
    TWA Station
  Denton, 76204

Washington

Eastern Washington
  University
  Showalter Hall-Room 117
  Cheney, 99004

West Virginia

Marshall University
  400 Hal Greer Boulevard
  Huntington, 25755

Wisconsin

University of Wisconsin-
  Milwaukee
  P.O. Box 749
  Milwaukee, 53201

University of Wisconsin-
  Oshkosh
  135 Dempsey Hall
  Oshkosh, 54901

DIRECTORIES

Following is a list of directories that may assist you in your job search.

Addictions and Recovery
  Resource List
Medquest Communications
  Incorporated
629 Euclid Avenue,
  Suite 500
Cleveland, OH 44117

American Network of
  Community Options and
  Resources
ANCOR
4200 Evergreen Lane,
  Suite 315
Annondale, VA 22003

Billians Hospital Blue Book
  Billian Publishing Company
2100 Parrers Ferry Road,
  Suite 300
Atlanta, GA 30339

BOSC Directory
  Facilities for People with
    Learning Disabilities
  Books on Special Children
Box 305
Congers, NY 10920

The Canadian Almanack and
  Directory
Copp Clark Publishing
  Company
Toronto, Ontario
  Canada M5S 1A1

Directory of Canadian
  Universities
  Association of Colleges
  and Universities of
  Canada
  350 Albert Street, Suite 600
  Altona, Ontario
  Canada K1P 1131

Directory of Juvenile and
  Adult Correctional
  Departments, Institutes,
  Agencies and Paroling
  Authorities
  American Correctional
  Association
  8025 Laurel Lakes Court
  Laurel, MD 20707-5075

Directory of Public
  Elementary and
  Secondary Education
  Agencies
  U.S. National Center for
  Education Statistics
  555 New Jersey Avenue
  NW
  Washington, DC
  20208-5651

Directory of Public School
  Systems in the United
  States
  Association for School,
  College and University
  Staffing
  1600 Dodge Avenue,
  Suite 330
  Evanston, IL 60202-3451

Pattersons American
  Education
  Educational Directories
  Incorporated
  P.O. Box 199
  Mount Prospect, IL
  60056-0199

Private Independent Schools
  Bunty and Lyon
  Incorporated
  238 North Main Street
  Wallingford, CT 06492

Private Schools in the United
  States
  Counsel for American
  Private School Education
  1726 M Street NW
  Washington, DC 20036